Four Meditations *on* Happiness

Four Meditations *on* Happiness

Michael Hampe

TRANSLATED FROM THE GERMAN BY
JAMIE BULLOCH

Atlantic Books
LONDON

First published in Germany as *Das vollkommene Leben* in 2009
by Carl Hanser Verlag GmbH & Co. KG.

First published in Great Britain in 2014 by Atlantic Books,
an imprint of Atlantic Books Ltd.

Further copyright information can be found on p. 243.

10 9 8 7 6 5 4 3 2 1

A CIP catalogue record for this book is available from the British Library.

Hardback ISBN: 9780857894038

E-book ISBN: 9780857894052

Paperback ISBN: 9780857894045

Printed in Italy by Grafica Veneta.

Atlantic Books
An Imprint of Atlantic Books Ltd
Ormond House
26–27 Boswell Street
London
WC1N 3JZ

www.atlantic-books.co.uk

A philosophical canon

For Hugo

‘Happiness is poor material… It is self-sufficient. It needs no commentary. It can roll up and go to sleep like a hedgehog.’

Carl Seelig, *Wanderungen mit Robert Walser*

‘Without a foundation in the conventional truth, the significance of the ultimate cannot be taught.’

Nāgārjuna’s *Mūlamadhyamakakārikā*,
Chapter XXIV, 10 [trans. Jay L. Garfield]

‘… all human life is radically deficient and a failure, if only because all humans in the end die, and thus fail to live up to the imaginary standard of continuing to last at least a bit longer.’

Raymond Geuss, *Outside Ethics*

‘It is an awful, an awesome truth that the acknowledgement of the otherness of others, of ineluctable separation, is the condition of human happiness. Indifference is the denial of this condition.’

Stanley Cavell, *Cities of Words*

‘In ourselves we experience a multitude in a single substance…’

Gottfried Wilhelm Leibniz, *Mondadologie*, Paragraph 16

‘Good luck, good luck, here comes the pit foreman,
He has already lit his lamp, already lit his lamp
Which shines a light
And leads us into the night…’

Traditional German miners’ song

Contents

Four Meditations *on* Happiness

CHAPTER ONE

The Calenberg Prize

The giant sloth

'Nobody gets out of here alive' – apparently the phrase had been sprayed on a wall in Hamburg. I heard this on the radio while having breakfast one rainy Monday morning. It was after I'd made the trip from Hanover to Pattensen to go to the Calenberg Academy for the first time in eighteen months. I had the feeling that I'd already come across this line – 'Nobody gets out of here alive' – in a newspaper advert for an action movie about inmates on death row trying to break out from a high-security American prison; in the end the heroes do indeed get out alive. But as a slogan sprayed on a wall in a city, I found it remarkably astute. Not warlike as in the advert for the film, but wise in an amusing way. Because to all intents and purposes this graffiti – if you allow a very broad interpretation of the word 'here' – is always correct. Although for a while we do get from A to B on the earth's surface, nobody gets out of this world alive.

As it is bound to come to an end for all of us – and probably dismally – we may wonder why we invest so much time and effort in changing and supposedly improving our so-called 'circumstances'. Perhaps our desire for change and improvement is merely an attempt to rid ourselves of the anxiety created by the (at least unconscious) realization expressed publicly in this graffiti. At the heart of our quest to make everything better might be the idea that we could perhaps avoid death, too, if only we tried hard enough to improve our circumstances. Maybe the realization that death is unavoidable seldom finds its way into our 'emotional centre', or whatever you wish to call the thing that makes us act in such and such a way when there's no time to think and weigh things up.

The need for change, however, varies in importance throughout our lives. Small children often want everything to be repeated. For example, they want the story that was read to them yesterday read to them again today. But with the onset of puberty – if not before – it's a different matter. It certainly was in my case. Not long after school, in my second semester at university, I suddenly became terribly depressed at the thought that my life would keep going on in the same way. I couldn't stand my home town, Stony Brook, any more and I'd hoped that everything would be different in Boston. Many people labour under the illusion that their life could be put 'in order' if they were only able to move it to the 'right place'. But wherever we go we're still saddled with our problems in that place and we have to cope with our own selves on a permanent basis. In my youth I, too, laboured under the illusion of the magical effects of changing location. But once in Boston I had to adopt a very strict daily and weekly rhythm to overcome the chaos and loneliness that marked the start of my studies there. I'd thought that if I made it to Boston from Stony Brook then everything would change. When I got there, however, I immediately plummeted into a nothingness.

I could only slow down this descent by regulating exactly what I did when. I drew up a timetable into which I inserted not only my lectures, seminars and sports activities, but also my reading and sleeping times, and even the times when I would go to the cinema or sleep. All detailed with the precision of half-hour slots. I regulated everything. After living this regulated life for two semesters I was struck by the horrific thought that *everybody* might be filling the emptiness of their lives with timetables like mine. 'There's no way this can be right. There's no way it can go on like this,' I thought as I sat in the wasteland that was my student bedroom. I decided to change *life* (not merely my personal one) and swapped subjects, although not just as a result of my brainwave. I changed from veterinary medicine to philosophy, from the goal of curing animals to curing humans. My new objective turned out to be an overestimation of the possibilities offered up by the academic discipline known as 'philosophy'.

Some of my fellow male students were well aware of the desolation of campus life, others less so, but it affected them all in some way or another. They would combat it with sex and the problems of communication associated with sex, or to put it more accurately: with a succession of girlfriends. Besides the illusion of the *right place*, young people also harbour the illusion of the *right person* you need to find in order to spend this life with them. In some people this illusion results in a persistent changing of places and partners; in others resignation because they cannot put up with anywhere or anyone for long. Although later I, too, got married, I'd long given up believing in the power of sexual and geographical circumstances to bring meaning and happiness to life.

In fact, nothing goes on *for ever*, not even a precisely planned day; *everything* comes to an end some time, for the individual, for *all* of us as individuals – as that graffiti on the wall makes clear – and, if the scientists are right, for us as a species as well.

As I was sitting on the train from Hanover to Pattensen on the day in question, staring out of the window at the rain falling onto the brown fields, I remembered that on one of my recent visits to see my daughter and her mother in Zurich we'd gone to the university's zoological museum. There it had occurred to me that my daughter's life would be over, too, one day. As this thought unfurled in my mind she was standing beside a stuffed giant sloth in the entrance hall of the museum. At first I had told her it was a giant *groundhog*; she had corrected me. She gazed at the reproduction of this large mammal from the Pleistocene era while I tried to imagine the almost endless chain of individual creatures that had already died and were yet to die, and the chain of already extinct species, together with those that were yet to die out. The Calenberg Prize question had just recently been set and, with this in mind, I asked myself, 'Why should we actually try to improve something? And for whom? What sense is there in striving for perfection, given the seemingly endless chain of disappearing individuals and species?'

And yet life is not about the perfection of an artefact, about creating an existential masterpiece. The fact that we get hungry again, that each meal is merely a temporary satiation of our imperfect state – imperfect because we are hungry – and that no meal satisfies us, makes us *permanently* full, hasn't ever prevented anyone from cooking good food or even eating in the first place. So neither should the fact that we die and die out – i.e., no life can represent the ultimate and eternal perfection – prevent anyone from improving, not to say perfecting their own lives. A good or fair life, even a finite one, is surely better than a bad or unfair life, particularly for those who have lived it. Isn't that almost a conceptual truth? After all, a delicious and filling meal is still a good meal, even if we get hungry again afterwards.

'So what is the sting of mortality, which supposedly makes all our efforts seem pointless, other than an existential sentimentality about finitude and mortality?' I thought, standing beside my daughter and the Zurich giant sloth. 'Of course,' I reflected, 'Beckett's image of us as frogs (or was it crabs?) being cooked to death in a slowly heating pot – which, unlike a sudden slaughter, nobody gets into a fuss about – this image has its aesthetic charm.

'But does it give us insight?' I wondered in front of the stuffed bullfrogs. 'Do we not feel sorry,' I thought as I caught sight of the preserved prairie dog, 'for the comedian Bill Murray in *Groundhog Day* when he fails in his attempt to kill himself, to put an end to the perpetual recurrence of the same day, which means for him there is no way out of the never-ending continuity of his Groundhog Day existence?

'We mustn't see mortality as just a threat,' I concluded back then. Nothing would be gained or perfected if our existence went on for ever, no matter whether it were eternal in a linear sense or an ever-recurring loop, as in *Groundhog Day*.

Looking from a higher consciousness with Krishna

So taking a more positive view, from a distance, one might accept Goethe's dictum 'Die and become' or, like Nietzsche and Bataille, approve of the 'wastefulness' of nature, which produces so much only to let it perish again, I pondered on my way to Pattensen. After all, the most terrible things vanish from life's stage as well. By doing this, however, you aestheticize existence, turning it into a drama which can supposedly be watched from the outside. But the fact is that we all have to play along with life; we cannot be mere onlookers. Even if we were among the most horrible and least desirable human specimens ever to have wreaked havoc on this earth, we'd still hardly be able to affirm our *own* disappearance from the perspective of participants. In truth, we have no external perspective on the conclusion of our existence. Thus the aestheticization of existence is not only an act of cynicism towards what we are looking at, but also a self-deception in which we identify with our immortal godhead who observes mortals as if they were players upon a stage, a self-deception which we will probably realize as such in the moment of our death, if not before.

The suggestion that we should view our life and death – as well as those of our nearest and dearest – from the outside, from a so-called 'higher consciousness', and see ourselves as acting out a role, seems to have first been suggested by the Indian god Krishna to Arunja in the *Bhagavad-gitā*. But in the twenty-first century we find this heroic-aesthetic ideal faintly vulgar. Even me, an old humanities scholar, cannot believe wholeheartedly in a Krishna or any other deity on a so-called higher level of consciousness.

For, given the facts of our existence in the twenty-first century, what is there to make me proclaim 'die and become' *à la* Goethe or Nietzsche? After all, we no longer go into battle against Achilles in chariots, but twist our ankle when we run for the bus, slip on the deposits left by the neighbours' dachshund, then get run over by a tram. If we imagine that in animal factories around the world at any one moment, thousands of pigs are blinking at the light from neon tubes operated by automatic timers, creatures who until they are made into sausages spend only a few, probably less than pleasant months of life being fattened in concrete bunkers, the question soon arises as to what sort of becoming and dying should be affirmed here. Should we see such events from a so-called cosmic perspective as part of an extravagant drama? It is probably true to say that the affirmation of the supposedly heroic drama of becoming and dying has always needed the willingness and artistic capacity to heroicize reality as well as deny the banality of living and dying.

Meditations

'If you think about it seriously, only incurable narcissists could possibly want to live for ever,' I said to myself as I made my way from Pattensen Station to the Academy beneath my umbrella, which was being pelted by heavy drops of rain. But I also know that my own profession, that of academic – just like those of artists, politicians and industrial managers – is full of individuals concerned, sadly, only with themselves. Their inability to love prevents them from being loved themselves; this in turn creates inside them an *unquenchable thirst for recognition*.

But these sick narcissists striving for eternal distinction and those who forever feel aggrieved – are they not merely exhibiting something which secretly torments *all* human beings? Would we admire their success otherwise? Does not the fact of death poison the pursuit of eternity and perfection *from the very beginning and for all of us* in a way which cannot help but make our existence seem miserable, forcing us to seek compensation in constant recognition and the immortality of fame? Is death not a sort of punishment meted out to us whatever we do with our lives?

Up until a certain age no child knows or believes that death exists. The first time they are confronted with death it is a shock. Is our quest for unending recognition and unending fame actually an expression of the wish for immortality, for a return to the modus vivendi in which we once existed as children? Is it not perhaps an illness in the sense of a deviation from healthy normality? This obsession with eternal status in the world is perhaps no more than the *honest expression* of what *all* people basically want *always* (even if mostly in secret): perfection, endlessness, and the constant attention of everybody else. Maybe the consciousness of death cuts such a deep wound in us all that it can only be patched up again with the religious illusion of eternal life or the pursuit of unending recognition. And the more people lose the religious belief in eternal life, the more they have to strive, almost frantically, for unending recognition.

Sometimes the attempts at perfection in my world remind me of the exercises performed by Buddhist monks in Tibet, India or somewhere else on Earth, who will spend days creating a complex pattern with brightly coloured sand on a sky-blue background. In the centre of this pattern is the wheel of time or Mount Kailash, which in some mythologies of the northern Indian–Tibet region represents the centre of the world. Soon after finishing their sand picture, or mandala, the monk tries to imagine the pattern in meditation – or does actually imagine it – before the Dalai Lama destroys the mandala in the so-called Kalachakra initiation. As I once saw in a Werner Herzog documentary, this involves wiping at the colourful lines of sand until they blur into a grey nothingness. The pile of sand is then shovelled into a silver-and-gold vessel. The vessel is carried to a river and the Dalai Lama tips the grey sand, which once had formed an unbelievably complex pattern, into the water.

This is an exercise in transience, the purpose of which I do not understand. Perhaps I don't understand it because I am not versed in the meditation they perform; neither the meditation of emptiness nor the imagining of a complex pattern with symbols for over 720 deities *after* the meditation of emptiness. Why should consciousness be exercised thus for transience, in view of the *fact* that transience exists whether we're aware of it or not? Does it make any difference whether our lives pass with or without an awareness of transience? This question asks what the sense of philosophizing is, if philosophizing means learning about death. But after decades of philosophy I still had to ask myself: exercises in mortality – why? Maybe Buddhists train for a better reincarnation. But if you don't believe in that sort of thing – a spiritual career spanning a number of existences – why bother training for it? Don't we train only when, after being provisional, things become serious and *final*, rather than when something simply stops which we feel is neither wholly provisional nor wholly serious and final? Are we not continually producing complex patterns of thinking and feeling which are then wiped out, not by ourselves or the Dalai Lama, but by an accident of some sort or a fatal illness?

Bloomsbury

It was not an obsession with recognition that led me into philosophy. I hoped that engaging with philosophy would bring me clarity and reason, allow me to reach an understanding with myself and lead a happy life – a philosophical existence conversing with like-minded people. Back then I was convinced that the academic study of philosophy would enable me to learn how to *lead* my life. But that didn't happen.

This hope had first surfaced at the end of my first semester studying veterinary medicine in Boston, when I met the friends of my next-door neighbour Edward. The party he was having meant I couldn't concentrate on reading *The Body Plans of Mammals*. At the very moment that I flipped shut my textbook in anger at the noise coming from his room, Edward knocked at my door to invite me to the party; he guessed I wouldn't be able to work with the music playing. The Chet Baker discs he always listened to were turned up pretty loud, and as Edward stood there in my doorway the wonderful 'My Funny Valentine' was blaring out. At this party – the first and only one I've enjoyed in my entire life – I met Leonard, a tall, gangly friend of Edward's. We got chatting and the conversation soon turned to the subject of 'good'. Leonard shared G. E. Moore's view – totally unfamiliar to me at the time – that although good was indefinable, it quite clearly existed in *friendship*. With great enthusiasm, yet unpretentiously, he told me about Moore's ethics and the Bloomsbury Group, about the friendship between John Maynard Keynes, Moore and Virginia Woolf. I'm sure it was not just the ideas but Leonard's charisma as well which made me go straight to the university library the following morning and borrow Moore's *Principia Ethica* and books about the Bloomsbury Group, rather than continue with *The Body Plans of Mammals*.

I never returned to *The Body Plans of Mammals*, but instead worked on the idea that the right life, the good and happy life, must exist in a *philosophical community* such as I imagined the members of the Bloomsbury Group once had. As I read more about the philosophical life, which usurped my veterinary studies, and became impressed particularly by Pierre Hadot's books on ancient philosophical communities, the Bloomsbury Group blended into the friends in Epicurus' garden and the members of the Stoic schools. And then I thought that to lead the right life I had to study philosophy, as those people in the philosophy seminars would also form similar communities dedicated to the right life, all of them helping each other in this quest.

My notion that university philosophy had some connection with philosophical communities of the past or the Bloomsbury Group or even practising the right life proved to be a false one, but I didn't realize this until I had embedded myself firmly in philosophy and the academic life. Although I never really stopped thinking that something had happened to me when I met Leonard at Edward's birthday party, it had nothing to do with my academic existence. In a sense, my involvement with the Calenberg Prize question and the papers attempting to answer it is a *return* to this conversation with Leonard. The various viewpoints which will become apparent in the texts that follow have remained viewpoints of mine and viewpoints that other people have plausibly advocated against me in public. The answers to the Calenberg Prize question were answers that I always believed I could find within myself or answers that I discovered in the outside world as an articulation of my inner indecisiveness, but which never cropped up in conversation between friends and me because I did not find such friends (if you don't count Kolk).

At university, like many young people before me, I wished to learn (with the help of others) how to attain reason in my life. But I also had to learn that at university the same unreason prevails, those same power games of so-called viewpoints or positions are played out as in any other place where a variety of people gather. It is always about who can emerge as the victor against another or several others. I, on the other hand, was convinced that Kafka was right in his 'Investigations of a Dog': all the dogs had to be coaxed to gnaw at the bone to get to the marrow. But where there is argument only about who gets the bone in the end, we don't achieve any understanding. That depressed me. It is largely a result of these social relations that I couldn't help viewing my life as a failure; and here I must describe my existence in the Academy, which was intended to be a path to happiness, but which actually took me in the opposite direction.

Curriculum Vitae

With the help of my tutor Hans-Georg Hauptmann I became secretary of the Calenberg Academy of Sciences. Before that I was chief assistant and a hopeful postdoctoral student of philosophy at Zurich University. My project was the history of semantic holism from Spinoza to Robert Brandom. When this project started I was convinced of the power of reason as it seemed to be expressed in the systems of Spinoza and Leibniz, but also in Hegel and Brandom. Then the project crossed the line between analytical and hermeneutic philosophy, which must have been my ulterior strategic motive, although I was unaware of this at first. Later, however, it was brought to my attention fairly emphatically by the departmental representatives in Zurich.

I had arrived at this project via a circuitous route. From studying the Bloomsbury Group, specifically the works of Moore and Virginia Woolf, I had switched to the critical theory of the Frankfurt School and to pragmatism. I thought, you see, that there must be a social reason for the fact that I was unable to find a Bloomsbury-like circle of friends at the Academy. With its totalitarian economic structures, society no longer permitted true friendship and a happy life, not anywhere, not even at university. Capitalism has tried to prevent the formation of happy communities, which have been the subject of philosophical inquiry ever since antiquity. For only in unhappy communities can the unremitting pursuit of wealth survive, as well as the suffering that occurs when human needs remain unsatisfied. Where people turn away from their own wealth and needs, opting instead for intellectual playfulness in the company of good friends, the economy is no longer so important, I thought. When I voiced this idea to my professor in Boston, he referred me to the writings of Max Horkheimer and Theodor W. Adorno, and their view that a good life was impossible where false social relations existed. I learned that in developing a critical theory the Institute for Social Research, which had moved from Nazi Germany to New York, had been influenced by American pragmatism and the relativization of the difference between facts and values. Thus I rounded off my first philosophy degree with a study of critical theory and pragmatism.

Both of these – the pragmatism of Peirce and Dewey, and the critical theory of Horkheimer and Adorno – are in turn influenced by Hegel's dialectical theory, while late Horkheimer is also influenced by Schopenhauer's pessimism. In order to study Hegel and Schopenhauer I learned German and came to Zurich, where I did my PhD in optimism and pessimism: reason as a principle of Hegelian philosophy and the will as a principle of Schopenhauer's philosophy. Although my thesis was highly praised and I was given a post in the philosophy seminar, they basically thought of me in Zurich as 'the American' and never stopped asking me about American philosophy. And so, ten years after I met Leonard, this Spinoza–Hegel–Brandom project materialized, by which time my original impetus for studying philosophy – to make my life and that of other people a happy one – had long been forgotten.

For years I was highly esteemed at the Zurich philosophy seminar as an American who had come to Switzerland from Harvard University in Cambridge, Massachusetts, to study German philosophy from Kant to Hegel and Schopenhauer, but who had then stayed 'for ever' in Zurich or Switzerland. Right at the very end, however, I was dropped when they *rejected* my postdoctoral thesis, a 972-page historiography of the idea that truth and meaning only exist holistically.

Teacher–pupil relations, professional and marital conflict

It must have been teacher–pupil relationships in philosophical communities which best corresponded to the ideal I cherished while still in Boston. These were the main model for friendships I had first dreamed of at the birthday party, when gazing at Leonard's peculiarly long face, which reminded me of a noble and melancholic horse. Teacher–pupil relationships: Socrates and Alcibiades! Gautama and Ananda! Epictetus and Arrian! The truth is, however, that life in academies and universities is full of hatred. My own experience was nothing unusual. For often an academic assistant like me is fixed for life in a position of dependency, just as an animal's skin is fixed by the taxidermist in an attack or searching position. The taxidermist had preserved the groundhog in his sentry position; my tutor, Hauptmann, had preserved me in life-long gratitude and subordination, first by ruining me academically with his negative assessment of my postdoctoral thesis, then with the Pattensen job, stuffing me in a gesture of gratitude. On the unhappiness scale, being stuffed with an indebtedness of gratitude to your superior is worse than dying. You suffer a terrible loss of freedom, because you can't stop thinking of the process in which you failed, and of those who drove the process and let you fail.

My tutor, Hauptmann, was a founding member and later President of the Calenberg Academy of Sciences at Pattensen. Only eight years after it was established, the regional government of Lower Saxony decided to close down the Academy, because, they maintained, this was the only way they could afford to finance the Hanoverian cluster of excellence for research into inhibiting aggression. I was given early retirement.

As a pensioner I focused mainly on reading so-called quality literature, starting with the works of Robert Walser, then the novels and plays of Thomas Bernhard, who became a natural guiding light of my early retirement. To begin with I enjoyed the closure of the Academy and spent very tranquil days on my own at the Maschsee in Hanover. On my own, because after I failed my postdoctoral degree in Zurich my wife left me, or didn't want to move from Zurich to Hanover, claiming that she couldn't imagine a ghastlier city than Hanover. I remarked that she shouldn't imagine Hanover, assembling all her prejudices about the city like a Buddhist monk recollecting a mandala in his mind, but look at Hanover as it *actually* was. Then she'd see that it was much better than its reputation. My remark failed to have the intended effect; it was taken by my wife as another of my 'typically vulgar comments'.

So she stayed in Switzerland and I had to finance the expensive flat from Hanover. In order to keep custody of our daughter, she filed for divorce. Since then my daughter visits me occasionally in Hanover, but mostly I fly to Zurich.

In the beginning I could hardly bear not to see my daughter grow up. The financial constraints I suffered due to my early retirement and the divorce were hard, too. But when I'd come to an arrangement with my daughter over my visits to Zurich and hers to Hanover, I calmed down somewhat. Then my mother died in Stony Brook. I inherited a not inconsiderable sum, which my parents had managed to amass from my father's salary and the flourishing sales of the pictures my mother had painted of the forest and the sea on Rhode Island.

My mother's paintings depicted the landscape in which I'd been happy for the short period of my childhood: the forest and the sea. My parents used to work from home, which meant they were always around whenever I wanted to speak to them. I told them about the squirrels, cats and birds that I'd seen in the forest, and the ships I'd seen at sea. It was only when I reached puberty that they became strangers to me and I hated them. When the topics of conversation we had in common dried up I found my parents artificial, boring and pretentious, caught up as they were in their world of books and paintings. And although I wanted to distance myself from this world of my parents, I was ultimately taken back to the scholarly environment by philosophy. I wanted to get away from intellectual life and art, become a vet and help cows bring their calves into the world and cure farmers' pigs of their coughs. But instead of focusing on animals I stayed at home after my last year at school and railed at my parents out of an unfounded sadness. Now they seemed alien and tedious, and within a few months the world became alien and tedious, too. It has remained so ever since. I began searching for something which ultimately I've never been able to find. But this talk of 'searching' is nothing more than a well-worn cliché to explain why I've not been able to be happy since the onset of puberty. It's something I don't understand: like a night that never ends it remains a mystery, just as other people have remained a mystery to me ever since.

When I inherited the money, all of a sudden I no longer had to deny myself a visit to the cinema or a restaurant, or the purchase of a new suit, and I was able to pay for the incredibly spacious period flat in Zurich where my wife and daughter continued to live after I'd moved out. Alone in my mansard, in a *Jugendstil* villa near the Maschsee, I could spend almost every hour of my retirement as I liked. After breakfast and an extended read of the paper I would take a walk around the lake. Afterwards I'd read some Walser, followed by some Bernhard. My inheritance meant I could go for lunch to the café at the 'Sprengel Collection' or the restaurant at the 'Interconti' opposite the town hall. In the evening I went to the cinema or the theatre. Films provoked reflection at least as much as books did, if not more. Suddenly I was thinking again after years without contemplation, following the rejection of my postdoctoral thesis. This is how I passed my days in retirement at first: a lonely existence, perhaps, but not unpleasant.

Saved by Kolk

At the point when I was in danger of running out of material to read by Bernhard I received a letter from Pattensen, from the one remaining employee of the Calenberg Academy. Gabriel Kolk, the only staff member to escape redundancy, was the caretaker of the building which was now being rented out for conferences.

In his letter, Kolk told me that there were several post sacks sitting in the meeting room, full of fat A4 envelopes. He invited me to pop in some time to see what it was all about. Almost all the letters were addressed to me: 'Dr Stanley Low, Secretary of the Calenberg Academy of Sciences'. Because of the cost he couldn't send them on to me, but he did not want to return the letters to the senders or destroy them. Kolk was at a loss as to what to do with them. I realized immediately what it was all about.

Two years before it closed the Academy had – and now I finally come to the subject at hand – organized a prize essay competition. If my suspicions were correct, the envelopes had been sent by academics and scholars submitting their entries for the Calenberg Prize. The competition's question was as follows:

> Can human life be perfected and, if so, in what way can people find happiness?

The guidelines had stipulated that answers should be essayistic and intelligible to all, rather than in a form corresponding to contemporary academic standards, which would be accessible to university specialists alone. This was the only way to realize the jury's aim of receiving answers with a broader appeal.

I read no more than a small proportion of the submissions all the way through. In most cases it was clear after scanning the first and last few pages that these were either completely uninspired, school-level treatises on the subject of happiness in present-day neurology, psychology, sociology, philosophy or religious studies, in essence outlining the current status of research in a particular field, followed by a brief personal conclusion adopting an uncertain position on their more or less meticulous summary. Or – and this was the other type of submission – people sent in so-called 'how-to manuscripts' in the belief that they could win the Calenberg Prize with a list of pieces of advice. Once in a while I was captivated by a study which didn't fall into either of the categories above, and then I'd read it from start to finish. I put these essays on a special pile, so I could read them a second time and in greater detail. I sat for a whole year alone at my desk – there was no longer any jury or committee to award the prize. But after a while I decided to put the best submissions in ranking order, at least *as far as I was concerned*, and at some point to make these public. This book is the result of that process.

Before I embarked on the submissions I must admit I had lost faith. I couldn't see the point of philosophical books any more, and I certainly couldn't see the point in this prize competition. The fact that some of them caught my interest didn't really change my mind, but I did start wondering whether *other people* might get something out of the essays. If Kolk had no major jobs to do in the garden, he would occasionally engage in conversation when he brought me a cup of tea. Sometimes he even sat down with me at the large conference table. I realized during our conversations that Kolk the gardener was better educated than all the people I had met up till then as a teacher, colleague or student at universities and academies.

As he told me in the course of one of our conversations, Kolk had studied maths, philosophy and geology in Heidelberg, Cambridge, Paris and Pittsburgh. He was then intending to do a PhD in maths at Heidelberg and had been set a problem by his supervisor which was a follow-on to Schwarz's Triangle Problem. After a year Kolk discovered that this problem had been solved long before and that his supervisor had set him on a topic where there was no longer any work to be done. Kolk was so furious that he turned his back on the university and began a gardening apprenticeship. Soon after abandoning his doctorate and while he was still in the middle of his horticultural training, Kolk decided to take part in a television quiz show and aim for the top prize. And he did, in fact, manage to win the jackpot of one million euros, since when he has been financially independent, although this did not make him give up his work as a gardener.

'Even before the maths disaster,' Kolk said, 'I realized that I'd never be able to pursue philosophy as an academic career, even though I preferred it to all the other subjects I'd studied.' For philosophy professors, Kolk asserted with great accuracy, were almost all quarrelling with each other, and even during his time they'd increasingly been losing themselves in ever more meaningless systems or historical questions. After his abortive maths doctorate, therefore, Kolk had left Heidelberg University and embarked on his gardening apprenticeship in his home town of Tübingen. At the nursery of Meister Böhme he'd met many wise and – more importantly – contented people, far more than at the university, Kolk told me. The decision to embark on a gardening apprenticeship, apart from that to take part in a television quiz show, was the best idea he'd had in his life, Kolk said. He found that raising plants was 'something right' in the best sense of the word. There was practically no end of things to learn about the individual plants and how they coexisted.

During his apprenticeship at the Böhme nursery, and even more so since his appointment at the Calenberg Academy, Kolk continued to study mathematical and philosophical problems in his spare time. In the holidays, as he told me, he takes geology trips to places such as Australia and Tierra del Fuego (where you can discover the most astonishing rock formations) to boost his rock collection, which was already impressively large, as far as I could make out when Kolk once invited me to tea in his staff flat in the basement of the Calenberg Academy. He felt he was leading an ideal life, Kolk said: he could study without being tied to the 'mad organization', as he called it, of a university, which would sooner or later wreck him intellectually and morally. He couldn't imagine a greater independence than as the gardener of the park at the Calenberg Academy. He took almost all the decisions relating to the park, and the forestry chief of the regional government approved everything he applied for. Seeing the plants thrive here made him happy, likewise his unfettered pursuit of philosophy and science.

Whenever Kolk spoke about his plants or his reading he radiated the same enthusiasm. 'Look how this elm has grown during the summer!' he hollered to me one September morning, pointing to one of the two handsome trees that bordered the entrance to the grounds like columns. I was walking along the gravel path from the drive to the front door of the Academy building, and he was outside with a book, as he often was when the weather allowed and he was not tending the plants. Kolk was sitting in his green work suit in the old white pergola and, as I noticed when I sat beside him for a moment, was reading the German handbook from 1763 on gardening by Christian Fuchs and published in Halle: *The Perfection of Life. Sensible Ideas on Breeding, Nurturing and Improving Plants and Small Animals in the Artificial Garden, with a Supplement on the Uplifting Effects on the Human Soul of Caring for Creatures*. The book was open at the chapter entitled 'How Trees, Fungi and Bugs Can Help and Harm Each Other, and How to Improve Harmony between These Beings'. When Kolk told me that he knew no greater text in the history of philosophy than Spinoza's *Ethics* he used the same tone and had the same glint in his eye as when extolling the delphinium as the plant with the most beautiful shade of blue. Before I met Kolk I wouldn't have believed that people like him could still exist: people who actually read books and think about them, rather than reading the books to review them or using a number of books to create another book, which advances them a step further in their academic career.

The selection

And so, now in retirement, not only did my hatred of university subside as a result of my conversations with Kolk, but my irritation at the philosophical–literary book business subsided, too. Taking my cue from my own reading of the better submissions to the competition (for the now non-existent prize) and from Kolk's attitude towards reading, I resumed my studying. This time I found I was focused and enjoying it. 'How many people in early or late retirement, and how many educated gardeners and cobblers read treatises and think about these essays while going for walks?' I wondered one afternoon in a flight of Walser-like idyll and forgiveness, having just re-read one of the more impressive answers to the prize question. The rays of the autumn sun shone through the colourful trees in the park, so consummately tended by Kolk, and fell on to the desk where I was working.

When I had found a publisher for the essays I thought were the best, communicating with the authors was a tricky business. It wasn't just a case of telling them how much I'd been impressed by their work. I also had to inform them that all prospects of a prize had vanished with the closure of the Calenberg Academy. Some of them wanted to publish their submissions alone and independently, without any association with the failed Academy and the abortive prize. I was able, however, to persuade four of the six authors who in my (and Kolk's) opinion had written the best essays, to have their work published in a volume. All I did was choose the texts I liked best, but strangely they *complement* each other, something I only realized when proofreading the German translations.

The first essay, by the physicist and philosopher of science Erwin Weinberger, seeks to improve life or happiness through the perfection of *things*, in technological processes and new methods of education. The second text, by the philosopher Lalitha Dakini, who deals with cultural comparison, looks at the perfection of the *mind*; it can also be read as a critique of Weinberger's paper. The third investigation, by the Chilean psychoanalyst Antonio Rojaz Marten, which we might call an example of cultural pessimism, claims that happiness is *impossible* and that no thought can exist outside of culture and life as understood biologically. It seems to me that Rojaz's essay tips Dakini's rejection of progress into a sort of nihilism. The fourth text, by the American sociologist James Williamson, ultimately views happiness as an experience that requires the *right relationship between things and minds*, which in his opinion fashion each other mutually, a relationship that guarantees a certain security of the person experiencing happiness, as well as making possible an intensity of experience.

These are four fundamentally different viewpoints. It is perhaps no coincidence that *unhappiness* and contemporary economic life play a role in all the treatises. The submissions that didn't touch at all on unhappiness and its possible social and economic causes seemed to me much more naive than those presented here. There were a lot more essays that sought the improvement of life in scientific and technological progress or in mastering the human mind. Likewise, Rojaz's paper was only one of many that denied the possible existence of happiness. I could have published four essays for each of the four viewpoints represented here. But on the days when I actually read the treatises that appear in this book – and for a while afterwards, too – I was convinced that each author was *right*. I digested their arguments and made them my own. This is why the texts impressed me; not just because they represented a particular viewpoint, but that they represented it *in a particular way* which convinced me this viewpoint was the right one, for a time at least. None of the essays reproduced here was written in German originally. Three were in English, one in Spanish. I translated them myself in consultation with the authors. The fact that I translated all the texts means there is a certain homogeneity in tone.

Kolk endeavoured to expunge the 'Bernhardisms', as he called them, from my introduction.

'Dr Low,' he said when giving me his impression of this text, 'your introduction is fine, I read it with interest, particularly those many things about your life I knew nothing of before. But the tone you use and your assessments of the essays – are they not a little too Thomas Bernhard-like? Don't you think that some passages sound like you're trying to get even with the people and relationships from your university years? Nobody will want to read that, apart from those people who are trying to get even, too,' Kolk said. 'You know that I also rate Thomas Bernhard as a master of language and hyperbole. But it's not possible just to go on with his voice. If I were you,' Kolk said, 'I'd get rid of those passages.'

'Do you know something, my dear Kolk?' I replied. 'I've never had my own voice. Throughout my life I've only ever written academic papers in that tone in which you write academic papers. If you want to be published in the *Archive for the History of Philosophy* you have to write in the way they write in the *Archive*, and if you want to be published in *Insight* then you have to write in a different way. They all have so-called *guidelines* for authors. You can't just write,' I said to Kolk, 'willy-nilly.'

'You don't write with your willy,' Kolk joked. 'The image doesn't work. That wouldn't have happened to Bernhard,' he said with a laugh.

'Whatever,' I replied. 'I don't have my own voice and I can't find one, either, just to write this introduction.'

'Well,' Kolk said thoughtfully, 'it would be a good thing to have your own voice, and not just for this introduction, wouldn't it?'

Stanley Low
Hanover
April

CHAPTER TWO

Scientific and technological progress as a means to eliminate unhappiness

Introduction

Our path to happiness lies in avoiding unhappiness. That is the first hypothesis of this study. The best means we have of avoiding unhappiness are science and technology: hypothesis number two. To understand and accept these hypotheses we must examine the progress of science and technology. If we imagine the process of science advancing *ad infinitum*, in some distant infinity we will be able to measure *everything*, even the degree of a person's happiness or unhappiness. Maybe this will take another hundred, two hundred or five hundred years. But the most positive view on the world that we know tells us that this is a *law*: it is a *correlation of variables* that vary in their relationship to each other. Our happiness, too, varies in relation to a number of factors which are at present unknown to us. There are elements of our consciousness and emotional life which are decisive for happiness. We will define these factors as variables and identify how they relate to each other. At some point in time *everything* will become unlocked to us. Mysteries will vanish. Finally, when reality – including our own selves – has become transparent, the scales will fall from our eyes and we will see how intelligible the world is fundamentally.

To substantiate this hope that happiness is dependent on our scientific knowledge and can be achieved with its help, we need to confront the critics of modern science, especially the critics of *progress* and those who pour scorn on scientific *truth*. This is our first task. After this we will imagine a sort of *utopia* to examine the possibilities of self-transparency and its consequences for human happiness.

Progress exists: what the history of science teaches us

Our scientific culture has existed for only 400 years. And it is only in the last hundred years or so that we have had a picture of what takes place inside matter and in the brain. If experimental and mathematical science is pursued for another 3,000 years – as long as an intellectual culture has been striving for knowledge and mastery of the world and the self, starting out with the less-than-suitable tools of myth, religion and philosophy – we will be able to recognize and, with technology, influence things and processes which today appear to be totally beyond our reason. Just as the phenomena of accelerated movement, light, magnetism, electricity and procreation were once considered to be *mystical* processes and forces, today consciousness and qualitative experience seem something quite apart from nature. Before Newton the magnet was seen as a living entity or as possessing a soul. Goethe still believed light to be divine, and around 1900 Hans Driesch came up with the idea of a spiritual life force to explain procreation.

When faced with something we cannot understand we resort to religious symbols and obscure philosophical beliefs. But the history of modern science has demystified these symbols and beliefs. For the world is accessible to our computing intellect. Most things which once appeared to be mysterious have now proved to be measurable and analysable. Thus we can infer from the past that everything which we do not consider measurable and computable *today* will at some point *in the future* be measurable and computable, just as those things which in the past we thought would never be measurable and computable are now fully accessible to our intellects. What accelerated movement was to the ancients, and magnetism, electricity and procreation were to the early modern period, consciousness and qualitative experience are to us today.

Nobody could have predicted the significance of infinitesimal calculus before it was developed by Newton and Leibniz. But calculating with infinitely tiny values allowed the human intellect to compute and understand accelerated movement, which to Plato and Aristotle had seemed mathematically unknowable. Likewise Galileo's telescope and Newton's gravitational theory eliminated the division between sublunar nature and the translunar, supposedly divine world. Mars, Mercury, Venus, Jupiter, the Sun – these once divine entities beyond the Moon – have shown themselves to be *bodies*: rocks or masses of gas. We have sent people and robots to these heavenly bodies and we generate energy in nuclear power stations because we have understood the core of matter, which is the same everywhere and does not come to an end anywhere in the world.

The understanding of *non*-divine light has allowed us to cure people surgically with lasers in the operating theatre and to heat our houses with solar cells. Knowledge of the nature of inanimate magnets has given us vehicles which move almost without friction loss. And the discovery of DNA revealed that procreation is a purely material process. Since then we have been able to identify and cure hereditary diseases such as phenylketonuria, and can even construct organisms to our own specifications.

There is no doubt, therefore, that science is in a constant state of progress. This does not necessarily mean that we should see progress as a movement towards *a goal*, towards *the truth* or *certainty*, but understand it as a movement *away* from the mythical, religious and obscurely philosophical, and towards the measurable, computable and technologically controllable. If we focus on the goals of truth and certainty it is easy to fall into the following misleading inductive trap: as all scientific theories in the past have proven to be false, our current theories will prove false in the future, too. If progress is moving closer to the truth, then this is something absent from intellectual history, which only shows us a succession of false belief systems to which in all probability our current beliefs belong, too.

In fact, however, we are moving away from more and more examples of misunderstanding and obscurantism. This is how we recognize scientific progress, by turning our gaze *backwards*, as we must do, rather than trying to target an abstract and imaginary goal such as 'absolute truth' or 'cast-iron certainty'. If I want to get away from Scranton, Pennsylvania, *every* movement which takes me away from that place, irrespective of where it is heading, is progress. Science wants to get away from the unintelligible, incomputable and uncontrollable. That is why any insight into scientific laws, any mathematical representation of a connection with reality, any technology which allows us to fashion the world or ourselves (e.g., genetically) as we wish, is progress. It was a mistake of Hegel (1807), Popper (1963) and Peirce (1965) to consider progress in the development of the intellect or in the sciences *teleologically*, seeing it as the movement towards a goal such as the truth or certainty. Today we know that we do not understand what 'moving closer to the truth' means as a designation for the supposed teleology of scientific development. But this is no reason for us to dismiss progress.

As long as we understand progress *teleologically* and continue to believe that we do not know what science actually boils down to, we will fuel relativism and cynicism. For if we cannot *banish* this moving closer to the goal of truth and certainty, critics of science will claim that all human belief systems are equally true or certain, or equally untrue or uncertain, because they cannot be compared with one another, they are incommensurable. By this token science can never be a way to find happiness, so long as happiness is dependent on an absolute truth which is fixed. Because we know that people *used* to believe they were in possession of the truth and were nonetheless unhappy, and because we believe *today* we are in possession of the truth and remain unhappy, *in the future* we will also believe we are in possession of the truth and yet will remain unhappy – such are the thought processes of those who wish to *abandon* the Enlightenment project.

But even if I do not know whether Einstein is closer to the truth and certainty than Newton, or both are in different places, equally distant from the truth and certainty, it is clear that Einstein is further from superstition and misapprehension than Newton, who still believed that gravity was caused by God and estimated the age of the world to be 6,000 years. This is as well known as the fact that Paris is further from Scranton,

Pennsylvania, than is New York. And even if I do not know *where* I am going, I only need focus on Scranton, Pennsylvania, to determine whether I am making progress in *getting away* from there. Likewise, I only need to focus on our *lack of understanding*, our *superstition* and the resulting *anxieties* which make us *unhappy*, and establish that these are what we *want to get away from* to see that in the time between Newton and Einstein we have actually moved away from them, which means we have made progress without knowing where science's journey is taking us.

If consciousness and qualitative experience – the things within ourselves upon which our happiness depends – are a puzzle and a mystery to us today, and yet we have managed to move away from the puzzles and mysteries of the past, transforming them into what is measurable and computable, and thus technologically controllable, we have every reason to believe that one day we will identify consciousness, its states and processes – including those states that lead to *feelings of happiness* – as something material which obeys scientific laws and which we will be able to control with technology. This is the *correct* inductive conclusion we must draw from the history of science.

It may be that along this path our understanding of matter will alter significantly. But that will not change anything of the methodology of the enlightened science project. For the languages of mathematics – which, since the nineteenth century, have far exceeded natural languages in terms of diversity and accuracy – and the implementation of artificial computer languages, and the procedures of experiment and simulation, will continue to be refined in structure and application, however we may conceive of the material world in the future. It is not the perceived certainty of mathematics which is key here, or the evidence gained by the process of experiment. Far more important is the fact that, over the last 150 years, a hitherto unimaginable number of formal languages have been developed in mathematics and IT for the most varied of purposes.

These languages are *problem-solving processes* that can be installed in machines. The process of experiment – which, besides computation, represents the other mainstay of enlightened science – is chiefly a process of *critique*. Good experiments are continually shattering established beliefs and customs. They lead to new knowledge, and new meanings are forced into old terminology. Expanding our knowledge through experiment allows us to distance ourselves from our current miseries, by changing the terminology with which we describe and explain our world, and adapting our thinking to make it more pertinent to the laws of reality. Thanks to the multiplicity of formal languages and the wealth of new knowledge generated by experimentation, science can turn itself more readily to problems which have not yet been addressed, by describing them mathematically and learning how to research them via experiment or simulation.

We need only consider all that has become possible in *systems biology* over the past twenty years as far as mathematics and experiment are concerned. The multiplicity of artificial languages, the processes of experiment and simulation, and the constant expansion of computing capacity today make calculable such phenomena as tides, the weather and animal migration, which a hundred years ago would never have been regarded as subjects for accurate research; back then people thought they could only relate to these phenomena via elaborate observation tables, country lore and a so-called 'good instinct', i.e., very imprecise and unverifiable.

It is only a matter of time before we will be also able to apply formal languages and far more experimental processes to the phenomena of consciousness and qualitative experience. Back in 1853 Hermann Grassmann, who had developed a theory of tides, tried formally to record our emotions with a precursor of vector algebra. This happened at a time when the rapid development of multiple formal languages – triggered by Gottlob Frege's and C. S. Peirce's predicate calculus and George Boole's *Laws of Thought* (1854) – had not yet begun and experimental psychology did not yet exist. Much has happened since, even though too little has been in the direction of a mathematized theory of emotions and states of consciousness. But just as there are few fundamental objections to experimental and simulated biology, there can be few arguments against research into emotions and consciousness using calculus and simulation. It is only a lack of imagination which could engender the belief that there are insurmountable obstacles *in principle* here. Anybody today who takes this view on consciousness and emotions is making the same mistakes as the philosophers of antiquity, such as Plato and Aristotle, who said that only the uniform circular movements in the sky could be registered with mathematical precision; for the rest of the world we would have to satisfy ourselves for all eternity with other imprecise methods – with the 'myth', as Plato says in the *Timaeus*.

If, however, we can one day mathematically describe and simulate the qualitative character of consciousness and our emotions, we will also be able to understand them as a *state of matter* – whatever we then imagine matter to be. Before we reach that stage, however, we need to examine more closely *what* it is we wish to understand and learn how to control.

Up until now we have contented ourselves with imprecise expedients for understanding and influencing consciousness and our emotions, such as colloquial speech, drugs discovered by chance, like alcohol, marijuana, etc., or autosuggestion and meditation. Because we are not even in the realm of scientific problem-formulation here, let alone precise problem-*solving*, a scientifically precise theory of emotions and consciousness still appears impossible. But just as we have learned to understand and control large chunks of the world – inanimate matter, light and procreation – we will learn how to understand ourselves scientifically as feeling and conscious beings, rather than just through everyday practices, and to control ourselves with the use of technology.

Our habitual and, in some cases, successful use of temporary solutions such as language, drugs, suggestion and meditation must not lead us into the erroneous belief that we have already reached our goal or that – in the case of consciousness and emotions – we cannot *in principle* get any further with the methods of the measuring sciences. There is no doubt that language is hugely underestimated as a means of influencing other people and reality in general. How often do you hear said that something is 'just words'? Are not political movements set in motion by speeches? Can a verbal insult not lead to murder? Is it not the case that a lawyer's address to a jury can decide on the life and death of the accused? There is a tendency to see 'only signs' or 'just language' on one side and 'reality' on the other, as if the signs were not something real. They are unquestionably real, however, in the sense of causal effect: something is said to another person, such as an order in the army or on a building site, and the person who has received the order to open fire or to operate a crane does shoot or make their machine lift a huge concrete block. But although it is something real, we very rarely make use of language as a tool that we understand, in the sense of knowing how it works. On the other hand, it is sensible to distinguish between those languages which have *developed* and those which have been *fabricated*. According to Vico, people can only really comprehend those things they have created themselves. With the creation of artificial languages and language machines, i.e., computers, people have achieved a new form of self-transparency. Because the 'evolved' languages are at best only semi-transparent to all except a few linguists, rhetoricians and poets, i.e., those who use them professionally, the effect of linguistic utterances remains hidden to most people, too. It is only with the development of artificial languages that people really master this system of influencing oneself and others.

This first happens with the artificial languages of mathematics and computer science. After all, a computer's printed circuit board is 'just' a sign or plan, too. But the printed circuit board is a sign that is transferred directly into a machine which solves particular problems. And the programming languages which are created to solve particular problems, such as the coding of an image or a tune in a computer, solve them within the semi-conductor system of the computer circuits: a particular optical or acoustic signal is saved *using these languages*. In such systems, where are the 'mere signs' on one hand and 'hard reality' on the other? The two are inextricably linked in the machine. The difference between language and reality is fundamentally meaningless, because language is a part of reality.

The linking of artificial language and computer makes it clear that there is *nothing* which is 'opposite' to reality, but that there is only *one* reality. Language and signs appear in it, just as do rocks, dogs and planets. The theory advocated by some so-called 'constructivists' that we have moved on from a belief in reality or so-called ontology, because we recognize that everything is a construct, is nonsense. What we make from signs is a construct, just as the car or building we make with the help of signs is a construct. That is true. But constructs are real. If the linguistic construct of a speech triggers a workers' uprising, it can hardly be described as unreal. If the constructed car which brakes in a bank of fog on the motorway causes a multiple pile-up, why should it be called 'a mere construct'? If a building whose design has been badly calculated collapses, burying many people beneath it, why should we treat the bad calculations and the constructed building any differently from the buttercup in its 'constructedness' and refuse to take them 'ontologically seriously'?

What is important for a thing's degree of reality is not whether it is constructed, but the extent to which we *consciously* steer the process of construction to solve the problem. Farmers who have been breeding crops and animals for millennia exert a technical influence on living things and attempt to 'construct' the ideal dairy cow or ideal pig. But until the discovery of DNA they had no idea of the *mechanism* behind this influence. For this reason they were unable to *construct* in a proper sense; instead they had to *experiment* to discover which offspring resulted from a particular cow and bull, and a particular boar and sow. But already in breeding we can see a technical approach towards the living being, albeit an unclear one, which is not in full control of what is to be constructively influenced: heredity. In the same way we exert an influence on our mental lives by means of speech, drugs and broad rules regarding behaviour. So when someone gets worked up and threatens to start a fight, we try to calm them down with words; perhaps we offer them a relaxing drink and prompt them to sit down. All this helps *a little*, sometimes more, sometimes less. But today we understand as little of the mental and neuronal mechanism behind these actions, which enable them in the first place, as farmers used to understand of the genetic make-up of their livestock and crops. As soon as we identify the underlying mechanism our ability to influence will increase exponentially, just as our capacity to influence technologically the hereditary material of living beings has increased hugely since DNA and its function in the germ cells of organisms has become known. The important difference here is not between construct and reality, but between an opaque reality which we cannot yet reproduce and recreate by means of construction, and a reality which is completely transparent because we have constructed it. To achieve our freedom and serve our interests we must strive to expand continually the sphere of constructed reality.

Our examples show that there is not a huge gulf between 'mere signs' and 'reality'. Likewise there is no gulf between 'nature' and 'technology'. Technology constructed by people is the *continuation* of the development of natural patterns. The hammer is the *continuation* of the human fist; the wheel the *continuation* of human (or, with draught cattle, animal) legs; the computer is the *continuation* of the human brain. Just as in natural *evolution* problems of survival are solved unconsciously by the mechanisms of mutation and selection, *we* consciously solve problems by means of construction, in which, for example, evolutionary algorithms that work according to the principles of variation or mutation and selection support the construction of materials.

Biological evolution should not be understood as a *higher development* in the sense of a teleological movement towards the perfect organism which is no longer mortal and can propagate itself endlessly. Similarly, the technological development we are consciously advancing is not a teleological one towards the *perfect* machine which can solve *all* problems. Biological evolution is an unconscious development *away* from a problem of survival and procreation. Because new problems of survival and procreation are always cropping up, no organism can be the *ultimate* one. Organisms are components that interact in their particular environment and, because they change, are constantly creating new problems for each other. In the same way, human constructs interact with each other and with the structures occurring as a result of natural evolution, such as the human brain. New problems are always occurring here, too, because the technological systems and societies in which they work change. Computers are adapted to the cars and aeroplanes which they control, and the cars and aeroplanes are adapted to computers; and human brains adapt to computers and new reading and control systems in cars and aeroplanes. Societies adapt to the changes in their members' mobility caused by the computer-controlled cars and aeroplanes, etc. We cannot imagine that that this process will lead to an *ultimate constellation* of an organizational, technological or social nature. As soon as the natural and technological development is considered in terms of the solution alone, this development becomes a movement away from the problems that have emerged in the past. But because this movement away always leads to new problems, there is no perfect final situation to this process. This seems to be the nature of the problem-solving of complex systems in complex environments. But although such developments are only movements away we can justifiably call them *progress*, because, after all, *more and more* problems are being solved. If the development has progressed, then things which once were problems are problems no more.

Those who seek happiness must learn to avoid deception as a cause of unhappiness

The question of happiness and the question of progress we have discussed above are closely connected. For we have just seen that the movement of progress is a *movement away from existing problems*. Exactly the same is true of the pursuit of happiness. It cannot be a movement *to particular goals* – a great love, great wealth, honour or power – but must be a movement *away* from what makes us unhappy, in the same way that the movement of progress in knowledge is not towards an absolute truth, but away from error. (It was an error by Popper to believe that these two movements necessarily have the same orientation.)

Unhappiness is where the person seeking happiness *starts out from*. People who are happy seek nothing; they do not wish to get closer to, or away from, anything. Perhaps in childhood people start out happy, but this changes when they become teenagers and young adults, when they try as hard as they can to be *somebody*, and when the complications of their sex life give rise to the problems of lying and pretence. The need to adopt an 'identity' leads to a movement towards something or the image of a somebody one would like to be. Desire for the other sex also leads to a process of searching which is not immediately successful. This is where unhappiness starts.

But what is the actual *cause* of this human unhappiness, which we need to examine like a *mechanism* in order to understand the pursuit of happiness in the sense of problem-solving? One answer is: the *fanaticism* of the search for an identity and the *habit* of lying both to oneself and others. What is the main source of fanaticism and habitual lying? Answer: the search for identity conducted with religious intensity, and the human inability to accept and communicate things as they are. Why do people resort to a religious search for identity and the habitual weakness of lying? Answer: because they have desires and are mortal.

Desire moves us away from *where* we are and away from *what* we are as cultivated beings. Death ends all searching: it puts an end to the happy as well as the unhappy life. Desire indicates that we are not what we *profess* to be in civilized life. Very few people would advertise their desires as their actual identity; we do not wish to be animals in pursuit of food and sex. In order to pacify the relationships between people, civilization forces us to curb our desires or – in the case of sexuality – to conceal them and suppress the competition they give rise to. Civilization offers us masks to disguise the fact that we are creatures with desires, and offers us ways to console ourselves vis-à-vis death as the actual end of life, either with religious fantasies or by hiding death away in the lonely hospital rooms of dying people. As we have known since Rousseau, civilization, suppression and disguise belong together.

Moreover, as soon as people start to understand death they realize that they do not want to die. This is why they usually develop the tendency to deceive themselves, to deny the obvious fact of death by resorting to resurrection and reincarnation myths and other fantasies about the immortality of the soul. Civilization provides people with this opportunity for self-delusion straight away. If we did not fear death from the outset and were able to get along with our desires in society without having to adjust, happiness would be easier 'to have' than it is actually to achieve. Most religions are nothing other than attempts to cope with our own desires and our death. But they do this at the price of having to lie to ourselves and others. Religions are particularly dangerous when they make their adherents fantasize to the extent that they discard their religious identity – with which they try to conceal their animal identity as mortal creatures driven by instinct – and behave violently towards others who do not think and act as they do, and thus who are seen as a threat to the wall of lies behind which they have hidden themselves and live out their lives.

But what can we do against fanaticism and lies, the religious and cultural pseudo-identity which denies our animal nature, and against human failure to face up to the truth? Answer: an honest quest for truthfulness, which takes place above all in *enlightened science*. Modern science – which, without trying to search for an absolute truth or certainty, uses an intelligence purified of emotions – is the most important collective school of truthfulness. The identity of a person who devotes their life to truthful research into the world and themselves is precisely what the Enlightenment posited as a *scientific or enlightened being*, in opposition to life in religious delusion. To seek one's happiness with the tools of enlightened science means to endeavour along the path of absolute truthfulness and not to be led astray by a belief in mysteries which reason cannot comprehend, such as the assumption of a 'resurrection of the flesh' in Christianity.

Once we have opted for this enlightened ideal of life, we must stick to the *scientifically established facts* and *our own capacity to reason* if we want to avoid unhappiness and be happy. We need to avoid illusions that satisfy authorities, rumours and desires, and learn to be suspicious of things that will ultimately *harm* us. For every enlightened person, *truthfulness* must be the first and resolute condition for all endeavour aimed at improving our own circumstances, the quest for happiness. If happiness consists in realizing our wishes by eliminating those problems that are an *obstacle* to these wishes in reality; we need to find out exactly what it is that has prevented us from realizing them. This obstacle is what we must distance ourselves from in order to be happy.

But to understand what it is that stands in the way of our interests we need to learn to see reality as it is actually constituted, which means being receptive to truth. To see whether our wishes can be fulfilled in reality and, if so, in what way they can be fulfilled, we must have a knowledge of the facts and accept these honestly. We can stand by the grave of a loved one and tell ourselves that their soul is supporting us as it looks down from heaven. Or we can stand by the grave and ask ourselves why the person underground is no longer moving, no longer speaking to us and can no longer be of support to us. The first person is kidding themselves and others, denying the facts because they are unacceptable and unbearable. The second person is trying to understand the facts, which does not mean that they accept them as irrevocable.

If unhappiness means that we cannot fulfil our wishes in real life, then in theory there are two ways out of this unhappiness: either we change reality so that our wishes can be fulfilled or we change ourselves so that we no longer have the same wishes. If death makes us unhappy because we fear it, either we need to make ourselves immortal or eliminate the fear of death. So we can only change reality or our wishes if we *know* how reality and our own selves are actually constituted. This is the basic position of the natural sciences and modern technology.

Postmodern humanities or cultural sciences, on the other hand, do not recognize the reality of scientific truths; these disciplines contribute to human unhappiness because they have nothing with which to oppose untruth and fanaticism (which is always an exaggeration and thus an untruth in the sense of its inaccuracy). To all intents and purposes they do not deserve the noble title of an enlightened 'science'. They have taken their leave of modern science and thus from the Enlightenment as a way of life. They are partly to blame for the irrational religious conflicts which have brought death and unhappiness to people over the last few decades. For they have concealed the fact that prosperity and the power of peoples, which are in the tradition of the European Enlightenment, are not principally the result of violence and exploitation, but originate in the actual structures of reality.

It is not correct that modern physics and evolutionary theory on the one hand, and creation theology or the belief in the resurrection on the other are 'equally' true, or that both are hypothetical. Anybody who takes religious propositions as statements of fact – in itself an error which ignores all historical and critical interpretation of so-called holy scriptures – that can be regarded as equally true or false must say: the assertions of modern physics and evolutionary biology are true, and assertions about the creation of the world by a personal god and about the resurrection of the body are false.

Postmodern relativism fails to consider the consequences of belief systems in life and people's actions. It regards the belief systems of science or religion only as relationships of propositions, as rigid propositional structures, and ignores their technical applications and practical implications for the pursuit of happiness. In this respect, relativism is no different from the old scientific theory of logical empiricism, according to which 'science' was nothing more (in an ideal scenario) than a formally correct inferential system whose empirical content was verifiable.

Epistemological absolutism and postmodern relativism are positions which those who play academic games of theory hold to keep them occupied. But neither have anything to do with human life outside of academia. Both logical empiricism (as the most influential theory of epistemological absolutism in the last hundred years of intellectual history) and relativism ignore the fact that modern science is tied up with an enlightened *way of life*, that science has *existential* relevance, that we *use* it to improve our circumstances with technology. Stephen Toulmin brilliantly exposed this error of logical empiricism and relativism, which he called the 'cult of systematicity', an error in common because relativism is a *reaction* to logical empiricism. As ever, the opponent has adopted too many false assumptions from his enemy.

In reality, the implications of whether we adhere to this or that belief system are very far reaching. Relativism cannot understand these existential implications because it does not even consider them. But the person who builds their life on false convictions, such as religious ones, who conceals problems rather than solving them, will become impotent and unhappy. By contrast, the person who is truthful to themselves and others will be able to translate their wishes into reality if they recognize their problems and find a way of solving them. This is why religion makes us unhappy and science happy. For religion throws a veil over our difficulties and consoles us in the face of our problems rather than trying to solve them. It is a comfort and a delusion. If we are seriously seeking happiness, we need to distance ourselves from *everything* that can mislead us into self-deception and into deceiving others. This includes distancing ourselves from the religious way of life.

Relativism and capitalism

The relativism of postmodernism is frequently praised for its *principles of tolerance*. People who advocate what are seen to be absolute truths supposedly become intolerant and promote enmity between others. In actual fact the postmodern principles of tolerance are nothing more than a part of the so-called *flexibilization of people*. This flexibilization deprives people of orientation and makes them unhappy, because people who are too flexible no longer know what they need to move away from to improve their situation. To say that it is only tolerant if you relativize your own standpoint and acknowledge an alien one as having equal validity generally means that you have as little conviction in your own standpoint as you do in the alien one – that you look at it from an *external perspective* and forget or ignore the fact that you depend on it in order to move anywhere at all.

Of course, in certain situations it is sensible to take an external perspective on your own situation, to allow you to see where the problems, the unpleasant things in your life lie. In such a situation it may be appropriate to look at yourself from the outside, as a historian or a doctor might do. But when you have recognized the problems in your life, you must identify with them as *your own*, to give you the strength to solve them. Somebody in an unhappy marriage, for example, may analyse psychologically why they are actually unhappy. If they stick with this psychological perspective on their marriage, they will not find the strength either to divorce or change themselves and their partner so that the marriage is no longer an unhappy one. This is why it is necessary to have a rhythm or a vacillation from the involved internal perspective you suffer in, to an external perspective from which you view your suffering, and back to an internal perspective where you solve the problems causing the suffering. Relativism, on the other hand, only exists as an external perspective on existences, not as an existential position.

The relativist says: 'Some people think it reasonable to torture people who threaten society, because they believe society to be more important than the individual. Others abhor such action on the basis of a different hierarchy of values with regard to the individual and the community. At some point value judgements must be made without these being able to be justified. Because community is a requirement for the individual to have a good life, but also individuals who act in solidarity are a requirement for the community, the priority of the community over the individual and that of the individual over the community can both be seen as right. But the choice of one or the other priority is no longer philosophical if philosophy only exists where there are justifications. Here it is no longer about justification but value judgements.' Postmodernist tolerance has to claim that the concept of individual human dignity is culturally relative, which is why you cannot force others to adopt it and to refrain from inhumane methods of interrogation.

It is well known that 'tolerance' lends support to despots' lust for power and abandons those who are tortured in police custody. Torturers will welcome this tolerance and continue to demand it from those who criticize them. The tortured, on the other hand, will insist on the truth of the universality of suffering and of human dignity. What tolerant people forget is the fact that 'we ourselves' in our own culture have *moved away* from the notion that torture might be right, in order to improve our lives. In this history of distancing ourselves from torture people have exchanged arguments and weighed these up. If we are a product of this history in our own culture we cannot simply throw these arguments overboard. Do we no longer wish to take this movement seriously, but merely devalue it as a path which we might *not* have gone down? Do we no longer see ourselves in the tradition of the Enlightenment? Is the principle of tolerance – for example, in the practising of religion – not an achievement of the Enlightenment? It may well be that in moving away from cruel punishments and torture we have not become happy, but we have learned to avoid a source of unhappiness. Why do the tolerant relativists no longer see themselves in this tradition? Answer: because they do not see themselves existentially committed to *any* tradition; they prefer to hover 'above things', having become mere observers of their own lives.

Rejecting the relevance to reality of each and every scientific truth – not only the so-called absolute or definite ones – is thus ultimately an *invitation to have no standpoint*, something which devalues the efforts we have made as individuals and communities to avoid unhappiness. In this sense postmodern relativism is part and parcel of modern capitalism, which aims to make us ever more flexible so that we become available as consumers everywhere, and hurry in any direction that producers of goods want to send us.

We are supposed to do *everything* we are persuaded to and to buy *everything* offered to us. We are supposed to forget our history which has developed certain preferences and dislikes. We ourselves are supposed to become exactly the same *pure possibility* that money is, so that business can be conducted ever more rapidly. If we preserved our character and the preferences and beliefs we have developed, i.e., if we remained the subjects we have become, who hold certain things to be true and others false, certain things pleasant and others unpleasant, in short people who still *run* their own lives, maybe we would not put the futon next to the flat-screen television and hang the golden Buddha above the hygrometer. Our lives are not supposed to be run by ourselves, but by those who press ahead with profit maximization. They have to make our lives into tools for their own purposes, thereby incapacitating us.

People who can be sold *everything* because they are *no longer anything* are better market participants than people who only consider consuming *specific* things because they still know existential places where they would never like to be, where they would never, ever like to get anywhere near to. 'Anything goes' and 'Anything sells' are two sides of the same coin. The postmodern rejection of the subject and the truth are the 'intellectual lubricant' of global capitalism, which is not interested in human happiness, but only in the global increase of profit rates. Both ruling ideologies – the religious identity linked to the hereafter and the non-existent identity of people made flexible by capitalism – are sources of unhappiness. They need to be replaced by the idea of an enlightened existence which is borne by the quest for the truth.

The value of truth

For more than 2,000 years philosophers have been reflecting on truth. In the last century Alfred Tarski showed that there is an answer to this question – in *formal* languages at least, but not in non-formal languages. The languages of the natural sciences as well as the physical languages are not entirely formal, even though they make extensive use of mathematics. For they refer not only to finely constructed relationships in the laboratory, but also to the reality of everyday life, which technology is forever changing. If Tarski is right, then the concept of truth in those languages that are continually changing and expanding is indefinable. But the fact that concepts such as 'true' and 'good' are indefinable does not mean that we can get by without them or ignore what they pertain to. And yet this is precisely what postmodern relativists seem to believe, and they tend to doubt the value of truth *at all*; indeed they even look upon the quest for truth as damaging. At this point there appears to be a parallel between religion and enlightened science: anybody who doubts the existence of God is in danger of dropping out of religion and religious life. Anybody who doubts the value of truth threatens to lose a rational relationship with the world, even their freedom, as Bernard Williams has shown. For anybody who believes that all truths are *constructs* which could just as easily be the opposite of what they are because they have no basis in reality, may not see any major difference between a 'falsified' CV in a Stalinist personal file and my CV as I recall it – after all, a construct is a construct. But as Williams rightly says, we see it as an *intrusion into our freedom* if something which we consider to have *really happened in our lives* and which we consider important is deleted from our CV for political reasons, for example. The fact that I was a friend of the Jew Scholem might no longer be desirable in an anti-Semitic phase in my country. However, simply to expunge this from my personal file so that I remain politically acceptable is something we consider a *falsification*. But how are we to distinguish truths from falsification if everything is a construct independent from reality?

There are many *simple* truths we cannot doubt, such as 'I was born', 'I will have to die', 'My teeth are harder than my tongue', 'The sun is bright', 'In 1945 bombs were dropped on Hiroshima and Nagasaki', etc. These truths are *not* constructed. They are self-evident. The atom bombs as artefacts were constructed, however. They are the product of fairly complicated physics and technology. If it is true that an atom bomb was dropped on Hiroshima, must it not also be true that there are certain theoretical assumptions about uranium, plutonium and the truths discovered by Otto Hahn about the splitting of the atom? But what are we to make of the notion that truths about the facts of nuclear chain reaction do *not* exist or only as mere constructs, but the fact of the *dropping* of the atom bomb as an act of war that results in suffering definitely does? How can it be that in some cases those people who consider scientific knowledge to be mere constructs, thereby eliminating the ability to distinguish our best theories from fairy tales, can at the same time assert that the technological application of science can cause suffering? Has a fairy tale ever caused as much suffering as an atom bomb? If, on the other hand, the suffering and the reports of it are true, then the technology which *caused* it and the theories which made it possible really must be true as well. Otherwise the 'match' between theory and technology would be a *miracle*.

In fact, we look for truth to cope better with reality. We know what is real on the basis of truths available to us. We know the truths available to us because we know what we can change in reality.

Arguments that technologies were produced using laws of Newtonian physics which then turned out to be untrue are ultimately sophistic because they ignore the limits within which Newtonian physics and its technological application function. Newtonian physics is *true under certain conditions*, and the technology which it makes possible continues to take place under these conditions and not at the very high speeds which the theory of relativity speaks of. But what sort of technology has ever resulted from the belief in a fairy tale? Under which conditions do the carpets from *A Thousand and One Nights* fly? Is there an astrological or parapsychological technology which works and has solved problems for us? Can we specify the limits within which it might be operative? Is there a technology which would be the application of the belief in the resurrection or of a miracle cure? The answer to all these questions is 'No!' We can only produce, construct something complicated and important for our lives when we know *exactly* – not roughly – and *really* – not apparently – how the things are actually constituted. Knowledge is true, substantiated ideas. Without truth there is no knowledge and without knowledge we cannot successfully change reality. Newtonian physics is substantiated and true; it is just that its sphere of validity is not, as first thought, the whole world given bodies travelling at any speed. If it were simply false, the fact that all engineers still have to learn it would be incomprehensible. If philosophy represented a concept of truth and falsehood in which the Newtonian physics taught at engineering college were false but useful, and yet this concept did not permit the false but useful propositions of Newtonian physics to be distinguished from the false but useless propositions of religion, we would have to conclude that this philosophy of truth was worthless as regards our need to know what distinguishes truth from falsehood. Anybody who obscures or abandons truth in this way will no longer understand why we are able to change the world using certain constructs, such as those in mathematics and the experimental sciences, and not others, such as those of fairy tales and religious narratives.

The complicated and significant elements of technological world change may turn out to be something horrific, as in the case of the atom bomb (which was created to prevent something even more horrific: the possession and use of this weapon by Nazi Germany) or something salutary, such as the smallpox vaccine. If we stop believing in, and striving for, the truth, i.e., seeking rational reasons which we can only discover by addressing ourselves to things impassively and intensely, then we will lose the distinction between pipe dreams and functioning technology, between delusional systems and science, and will no longer be able to understand how we can relate to the world *at all*. And I mean a *successful* relationship with the world, especially on a *technological* level, which allows us to adjust the world to our needs, and avoid the suffering and unhappiness that exists.

Enlightened science created powerful modern technology because it was able to develop true theories. The reason why this did not occur in cultures dominated by religion was because these cultures knew too little about reality as it is in truth and were thus unable to influence it. If theories, religious myths and fairy tales were all constructs to the same effect, if everything were dependent on us, any beliefs people had would be irrelevant to their lives. Either nothing or – just as long as they believed in something strongly enough – *everything* would have to have technological consequences. But, in reality, religious faith does not move mountains, whereas dynamite, developed using true chemical theories, does.

As we can see, most unhappiness in human life derives from the fact that we paint a false picture of reality, that we fail to see it as it is because we are *afraid* of the facts. We are afraid of getting ill and thus we fancy that we could never get ill, only other people. We are afraid of dying and so we refuse to contemplate the fact that we have to die. But when illness or imminent death can no longer be denied, we fall into despair. On a psychological level it is the same as someone who would rather not know how little money they have in their account, but who spends gleefully and then falls into despair when they have to stand trial for indebtedness. The fact that not everything depends on us, because we have to *strive* to turn our wishes into reality, is *in practice* indisputable, irrespective of what we choose to believe as a philosophical theory of the truth. In practice there is no doubt that a reality independent of us exists, guiding us in our cognitive processes and by which we *must* be guided whether we like it or not. Sometimes it confronts us with resistance, sometimes it offers us security. The theorists who argue that *everything* is a social construct are no longer able to distinguish between what we can conceive of in any old way we like and the theory derived from an experiment which turned out thus *and not any other way*. This is why the concept of truth has no relevance for them, except maybe in the case where truth is understood as what we have agreed on. The history of science then becomes a history of beliefs which we have agreed to accept at a certain point in time owing to a certain 'style of thinking'. Later, because the 'style of thinking' changes, we abandon this consensus and agree on new beliefs. This leads to a so-called 'paradigm shift' or a new 'episteme'. According to the relativists, the proponents of different paradigms no longer understand each other because the concepts they use have totally different meanings. But this has not been the course of the history of science. Postmodern theorists, who no longer believe in the possibility of truths shared by people from very different eras, often point to the supposedly *large* number of different beliefs which people have already accepted as true and later rejected as false. They bring up the same old examples, such as Stahl's phlogiston and Maxwell's ether of light dispersal, chiefly to show that *objective existence assumptions* in science do not last long. The fact that we no longer picture ourselves using the words 'phlogiston' or 'ether' is supposed to be proof that today we live in a *completely different world*, one in which there are different truths from those in the world inhabited by people from the past.

Set against these same old examples, however, is an enormous chunk – indeed, the *majority* of scientific beliefs – which, within certain parameters, have retained their validity to the present day. Pythagoras' theorem has held true ever since Pythagoras came up with it. Not even non-Euclidian geometrics have altered it one bit. Similarly, the laws of the lever have held true since antiquity and have been taught in schools for centuries. Maxwell's equations continue to be taught, even though we no longer believe in the existence of the ether. Newtonian mechanics are still learned and are an indispensible element of engineering studies, even though much has changed since Newton's *Principia* and we no longer believe that physical reality is simply determined by particles, empty space and gravitational force.

The longer modern science continues its work, the clearer two things become. *First*, we see that mathematical formalisms of successful theories often have a universality that extends beyond their original applications; for example, when the mathematics that was introduced to record Brownian motion is used to describe the spreading of a virus in an epidemic. *Second*, as we have already seen, the experimental method represents an ongoing *critique* of science, weeding out from our belief systems those assumptions which appeal greatly to people's emotional bias, but which have not proved to be sustainable when subjected to experiment. If all truths were constructs there would be no sense in denouncing as falsifiers those scientists who arrange their experimental systems in such a way to produce exactly the findings they desire, and excluding them from the scientific community. An experiment is only a verifying mechanism if we allow it to run its course with *autonomy* rather than looking on it as entirely our construct.

An experiment can only deliver *new findings* and *challenge* an assumption if there is a reality present which is autonomous and resistant, rather than it being a mere showcase for our ideas and beliefs. New discoveries in technology are the results of new discoveries in experiments. Moreover, the requirements of the *repeatability* and *measuring accuracy* of experiments in the process of the development of modern science have become more rigorous. An assumption which has been *confirmed* by experiment is hardly likely to be rejected as false, even if over time the conditions of the experiment show themselves to be less generalizable than originally thought. But why is there so little acknowledgement that the representation of reality in the resistant and innovative experimental system is the best way we have of getting to know the world?

Search for intensity as a cause of delusion

The reason might be that facts are mostly *boring*. Especially if you want to know and measure them *precisely* to seven decimal places, as is necessary for some technical procedures. The process of knowledge acquisition via facts is not often exciting or associated with emotional intensity. Most of the time it consists of dry work with painstaking attention to detail. But there is a human need for emotional intensity, for suspense, excitement, meaning. It is believed that the human nervous system, especially the brain, is a sort of 'amplifier' of the energetic intensity of marginal physical processes. The result of this 'amplification function' is subjectively an intensification of experience. So if there is already an 'in-built intensification function' in our bodies, it is easy to understand why people are on a constant search for new, more intense experiences, why they find it difficult to remain in a less intense state of experience.

When people exaggerate or lie they probably do it just as often to produce intensity and meaning as they do to gain some sort of concrete material advantage or to avoid a similar disadvantage. Besides our poor ability to admit to ourselves the truth of undesirable facts, this is the main reason for the untruths of religious and political fanaticism, both of which contribute equally to people's unhappiness and join forces time and again, such as in the National Socialist 'movement'.

What is it that Carl Jacob Candoris, the mathematician, says so aptly in Michael Köhlmeier's novel *Occident*? 'People were bored . . . And National Socialism was . . . exciting. Every day a holiday. And full of meaning as far as the eye could see. Everything meant something: nobody knew what it meant, but everybody knew that it meant something. Meaning is like a drug. You don't want it, you need it. And you need more and more of it. Everything had meaning. And a higher meaning as well. Soon you're unable to speak without raising your voice. Listen to the radio broadcasts from back then! The topic couldn't have been more banal, but it was spoken in a tone as if it were *Parsifal*. Prophets stare back at you from the simplest passport photos.'

Of course, meaning, excitement and intensity are quite different concepts. The intensity of a love, the meaning of a prophet's religious words and the excitement of a crime novel are very different things. And purists will repudiate the idea of an 'exciting church service' (even though these days almost everybody talks of an 'exciting' rather than 'interesting' scientific lecture, as if science were all about entertainment rather than truth). But the intensity of love, the meaning of religious action or the religious word and the excitement of a narrative have something in common: they allow us to forget the banality and greyness of everyday life and facts, almost to the point where they disappear. At the same place in the book Köhlmeier has Candoris say that 'war and bombing' were 'exciting'. The *state of emergency* is sought because it puts an end to boredom, meaninglessness and the *lack* of intensity, and corresponds to what is clearly an almost organic tendency of living things towards intensification. When people who have survived a war talk of their wartime experiences, even if they were bad, they almost always talk of something extraordinary and significant. This is why so many people search for a 'great love' and enjoy losing themselves in a state of delirium or religious profundity without considering the often unpleasant consequences. For all of this satisfies the need for intensity. It is also probably the reason why people deny the truth and what is obvious, the self-evident, or why they simply put it aside and prefer to believe that something improbable – a fairy tale, an exaggeration, a conspiracy theory – represents reality. A religious movement can all of a sudden change much in people's lives: they believe that a *new era* is beginning and now they are engaging with the things that are *actually important*, whereas previously everything was just 'banal'. Given this, it is not strange that on the one hand many people dispute the facts of scientific progress, while on the other more and more people seek to rejuvenate their lives in religious movements. Admittedly, the modern Enlightenment started as a movement that promised to bring true progress rather than the apparent progress promised by the religions of salvation. But the path of Enlightenment is slow and boring, involving many generations of commonplace and painstaking laboratory work to produce results, whereas the path of religions and political ideologies is quick and exciting, supposedly leading to its destination in a single lifetime. Nothing has disproved scientific progress and confirmed religions of salvation, it is just that the slowness of scientific work and the lack of sensational meaning have made the Enlightenment unattractive.

Evidently the truths of science do not sufficiently satisfy our need for emotional intensity in our experience of the world. This is why most people prefer to believe in a divine figure in heaven and are prepared to go to war for it. Many people have a notion of happiness that entails a certain emotional intensity in their lives, even if this is a struggle between life and death. A life spent in research may be adventurous and emotionally intense. Only few, however, experience the discovery of a truth in the research process, and this experience is of only short duration in relation to the long and painstaking research dedicated to its preparation and evaluation. Once the truth has finally been established, the compliance of sticking to the facts alone seems to respond so little to the imagination and need for intensity that some people cannot help diving head first into a sea of illusion. If these fantasies interfere in people's lives via religious belief systems or political ideologies, they can sooner or later lead to unhappiness, as we have seen from the history of totalitarianism and wars of religion.

People's need for intensity is thus in itself a problem which needs to be solved *scientifically* and *technologically* if we want to progress on the path away from those factors that cause unhappiness in human life. Either we have to modify our everyday lives, which lack a certain 'kick', so that the basic human need for intensity is satisfied, or the need itself must be 'stifled'. This striving for intensity, this quest for intense stimuli may come from a time when behind every bush lurked a predator, the indications of which had to be amplified in order to be able to anticipate an attack. But this satisfaction must not lead to the unpleasant and unhappy-making consequences that war or compulsive gambling lead to, or whatever else human beings do to intensify their lives. Sport and games in virtual worlds may offer untapped potential here. The differences between the various strategies, however, are considerable. Whether I stimulate my senses with drugs to increase the intensity of my perception, or dampen it so I cannot feel the lack of intensity – so-called senselessness – whether people enter virtual worlds or wars, or ultimately lead their judgement astray with religious systems and political ideologies, so that intensities are produced in 'real reality', which thrust countless people into unhappiness – all this makes a not inconsiderable difference. The most important problem in this regard, therefore, is *how* the need for intensity can be satisfied without creating an addiction to the thing which provides intensity, and how sense and significance can be produced without damaging our ability to perform the everyday tasks in our reality, which is often banal.

Solution

What does progress on this path essentially look like?

It is clear that a study which no longer sees happiness as a goal of human life, but regards its attainment as the constant *movement away from unhappiness*, cannot give a simple answer to the question of attaining happiness. In the history of human existence new problems are continually arising which in each case can be solved by the tools of science and technology. This is why 'happiness' does not exist in this study (just as 'the ultimate truth' does not). In spite of this there are certain constants of unhappiness in human existence which have already been suggested and now need closer examination. These constants of unhappiness are: *death*, *desire* and the *need for intensity*. Before we can address these issues, and having reached a consensus on the idea of progress, we need to analyse in greater detail what we mean by 'solving the problem'.

If I have a tumour in my bowel, that is a fact. It has no deeper meaning. It has not been sent by God as a punishment. It does not express my secret or unconscious desires. It is not my way of expressing myself and fashioning something, as misguided psychosomatics such as Viktor von Weizsäcker would have us believe. Maybe I ate a charred, fatty bratwurst at a birthday party some years back, thereby ingesting a large amount of nitrosamine. Then there may have been an inflammation and cancer cells formed. Perhaps my immune system was fairly defenceless as a result of stress and insomnia. The cells embedded in my bowel mucosa and the tumour developed. Nothing but a boring, random convergence of certain circumstances. But the fact that I might die, that is of *great significance*, for me at least, and can be a source of unhappiness for me. (And significance is always significance *for* someone. This is why there is no significance in nature, because nature exists *for itself*, not for someone.)

The fear of death is of great intensity; like love it is an exceptional emotional state. But it is an *undesirable* one. Chit-chat about a cousin's bowel cancer still has a pleasant intensity, like an exciting hospital novel. But if I am affected *myself* I would rather return to grey, unexciting normality, which all of a sudden no longer seems so boring.

If the cancer should disappear and I do not die, then nothing is gained by a search for deeper meanings, only a precise knowledge of the facts. The tumour is clearly not a thing of thought. It has not been constructed by the doctor's diagnosis equipment, but grown unnoticed in the dark cavity of my belly. When I felt the pain in the right-hand side of my lower stomach, even before I went to the doctor and he switched on his ultrasound device, the growth already had a history which nobody knew until then, let alone could have told, but which had occurred. The operation shows the results of this history: the tumour and the tissue around it which may have been destroyed over a number of years. It is not something that stands for anything else. It is what it is, a naked fact which few philosophers today wish to believe in unless they have it in their own belly and the pain forces them to accept it as a fact, thereby becoming unhappy. If I die, I will not die because of a symbol or a meaning, not because of a construct of the diagnosis equipment, but because of the *fact* of a tumour. If I do *not* acknowledge the fact of the growing tumour, it will definitely kill me. If I do acknowledge it, I can start doing something *about* the tumour. On the condition that I have worked out *precisely* what it is doing. I can only solve the problem of the disease when I acknowledge it as a fact and research it in great detail.

News about the growth of the tumour in my bowel will make me sad, unhappy perhaps. This is why I have to do something about the tumour. For I do not want to be unhappy. What I can do about it depends on my *power*. The question of power over the tumour goes like this: do I have a technology allowing me to stop the tumour's growth, to eliminate it without my being fatally harmed in the process? Only with scientific and technological research is it possible to answer this question in the affirmative.

The second stage after *accepting* the facts is thus to *change* the facts if they make me unhappy. Both of these can be problematic. Accepting the unpleasant, possibly gruesome facts is a problem for those facing them. Changing the facts is a problem for those who come up with technological solutions. The problem we need to solve if we want to make progress in avoiding unhappiness is to acquire the ability to see things as they are, so we can develop the power to change them to how we want them. These are the two stages on the scientific and technological path of the Enlightenment to happiness.

With this approach we have already substantially extended human life expectancy by introducing hygiene measures and lowering child mortality rates. We have acquired the power to prevent unwanted pregnancies and to feed billions of people, which would have seemed unthinkable 200 years ago. We can fight infectious diseases, transplant organs, make deaf people hear again with artificial middle ears, construct hand, arm and leg prostheses, which allow people with damaged limbs to grasp and walk. We will learn how to cure blindness with an artificial retina and make paraplegics walk again by synthesizing the nerve-growth factor. The blind will see, the deaf will hear and the lame will walk; not because they have suspended their reason and believe in a miracle, but because people in thousands of laboratories are indefatigably in pursuit of knowledge, and technicians are making use of this knowledge for the benefit of all.

This process began more than 500 years ago when, following Archimedes, Galileo revived and developed the experimental method of acquiring knowledge. If we apply this process to ourselves we will be able not only to adapt reality to our needs, but to adapt our mind to reality. We shall become masters of our moods, emotions and thoughts. We will wipe out depression, delusion, poor memory and excessive aggression. Just as we help the stomach digest with artificial peptides when it is weak, we will anaesthetize nerves when nagging pain drives us mad. Likewise we will use suitable substances to assist the brain when it is too weak to remember or motivate us, or when we see ourselves incapable of accepting a fact. As long as we strive honestly for knowledge, guide ourselves using facts and recognize our freedom to live as we ourselves see fit, based on the knowledge we have, this process of the Enlightenment, the self-determination of our existence via knowledge, will continue. As the solution to the problem, it will be the path that leads us ever further from unhappiness.

But now to the three concrete problems cited above: death, desire and intensity.

Fear of death

One of the elements of growing up is learning to see yourself 'from the outside' and not confusing your fantasies with the facts. We marvel at children because they really seem *to see* what they imagine in their games, but this capacity also causes them fear. For the intensity their life has as a result of their highly vivid imagination and a not-yet-fully-developed ability to distinguish this fantasy from reality is an intensity of both joy and fear. No adult can ever derive as much pleasure from role-playing as a child who pretends to be a pirate or knight and dreams up a sea monster or dragon. But nor will an adult feel as much fear as a child in a dark cellar or in the forest. And yet distinguishing facts from fantasy, not merely viewing ourselves and the world from our own perspective, but from many and from 'outside', until we finally see the world as it really is – this is a process which as a rule we never fully complete. Faced with the facts of death we are generally unable to take this step towards objectivity. But in view of death we must learn to grow up if we want to be happy.

From a *functional* perspective, the view not only of modern biology, but also that taken by the seventeenth-century philosopher Baruch de Spinoza on this question, thinking about death non-stop, and especially the *fear* of death, is completely dysfunctional, irrespective of whether it appears to be imminent. This sort of thinking diminishes our will to live, and the mind-set that gives rise to such thoughts and fears might, if it is genetically determined, be under evolutionary pressure. For nothing which permanently impedes the organic activity of a living being, such as imagining death, can ever be beneficial from an evolutionary standpoint. If, on the other hand, death is irreversibly close, then fearing it no longer has any biological function either. Fear of death has a biological purpose only where there is an unequivocal danger of death, but where it can still be avoided.

Biologically, fear is an alarm reaction which can prompt and encourage rapid action, thereby preventing the demise of the creature seized by fear. Panic puts the body into a state of excitement, which allows the individual to make a quick escape or offer serious resistance to the enemy. Sometimes the release of too much adrenaline can also cause a temporary insensibility to pain, which allows the threatened creature to fight on or flee in spite of injury; both of these can save the threatened creature's life. Living beings which have exhibited a reaction of panic in the face of a great but avoidable danger have been advantaged on an evolutionary level. They have survived, whereas those who stayed calm, were not alarmed and continued to feel pain as they did prior to being threatened with death, were the ones eaten and unable to reproduce. In this respect the fear of death, if it is genetically determined and associated with specific physiological alarm reactions, may be positive for evolution.

Jankélévitch says that we 'find it hard to imagine what a metaphysics of death might be, whereas a "physics" of death is easily imaginable. It does not matter whether this physics is in the sphere of biology, medicine, sociology or demography, because death is a biological phenomenon like birth, puberty and the aging process; mortality is a social phenomenon like birth rates, marriage status or criminality.' Although the author of these lines quickly rejects this view of things as too simple, banal, it is the right one. Death is not, as he thinks, an 'absolute tragedy', a 'complete annihilation', an 'empirical–meta-empirical monstrosity' and a 'secret'. It only seems to us to be so from our immature subjective viewpoint. But our childish subjective viewpoint distorts reality.

Just as a child who is afraid of a man with a beard or who panics when they glimpse a shadow at nightfall, the thought of our own death troubles us and stirs the imagination even if it is not imminent. A child's imagination allows them to envisage anything when they see the beard or the shadow, whereas in reality these are just hairs on a chin or the light of the setting sun casting a dark image of the branches on the forest path. Maybe in the bearded man the child sees a bear wanting to eat them up; in the shadow of the boughs a huge black hand making a grab for them. They do not see things as they are, because they do not yet have *experience* of beards and shadows. The same is true of death for people who are not children, but have not fully grown up. Most people have not learned to keep their individual and collective fantasies in check when it comes to the phenomenon of death. For unlike with the bearded face or tree shadows on the path, with death it is *impossible* for the individual to learn through repeated personal experience to control their own imagination in these situations. We only die once and so cannot practise this experience.

But because we have no personal experience of death to teach us how it is to die, we imagine everything possible when we see a corpse and consider the question of what it must be like when we ourselves are in this state. 'We are attracted by the very things which frighten us . . . the moth and the candle flame, human beings and death – in both cases there is a similar power of attraction.' It is the intensity of the light and the intensity of the shudder we feel when faced with a corpse which unleash the attraction and get the imagination working (at least for human beings and death – what do we know of moths?). As suffering, social beings *we* cannot ever be in that state of death. And maybe the reason for the fascination with death is precisely its social impossibility. In any event the imagination of what will be harbours not just something frightening, but something *secretive*, too, and like all secretive things in our imagination this adds to the *intensification* of our lives. This is why there are so many stories about life in hell or paradise after death. These imaginings have the function which today is performed by horror films or fairy tales about blissfully happy states of paradise; they make our life more intense. In reality, we never enter these films, whereas one day we will inevitably face the situation of death, and then the question will come as to whether what actually happens will be *what* we have imagined death and dying to be or what others have told us happens, which they can only have imagined, because, after all, no one has yet come back from the dead. When the time has come for us to die and we start panicking, apart from the 'biologically programmed alarm' we become victims of our past fantasies, our own as well as those of others, which we have adopted in our culture.

There are reports of people who have almost died or actually did die and who were then revived – these 'near-death experiences' forming the 'basis' for much speculation about life and death. Let us examine this for a moment. Some people talk of how, when plummeting from a mountain or during cardiac arrest, they had a series of memories relating to their lives which went all the way back to early childhood. Ultimately, some saw themselves dying from above and afterwards had a so-called 'tunnel experience'. They appeared to be moving through a shaft, at the end of which was a light they were floating towards.

The Hungarian writer Péter Nádas had experiences like these when he suffered a heart attack, and he wrote about them in his book *Own Death*. Nádas describes how when he was revived he felt as if he were being drawn by a force through a ribbed tunnel and moving towards a light shining through an oval opening. He gives the following interpretation of this overwhelming experience: 'The oval opening was my mother's parted outer labia, which I knew from the viewpoint of the birth canal . . . They were spread apart and got wider the nearer I came to being born.' The strange light he was moving towards was 'the light on the maternity ward, filtered through opaque window panes'. A peculiar, bird's-eye perspective on their own physical state occurs in people who remain rigid in a single position for a long time. It is an illusion experienced by pilots on intercontinental flights, who all of a sudden seem to view themselves from outside; and people who meditate in the lotus position for hours can also see themselves from above. The rigid position in which most dying people are stuck possibly leads to this very illusion of observing oneself from above, something Nádas experienced, too. Other neurological processes might trigger a rapid 'playback' of life memories so that in the end, if Nádas is right, we might arrive at a recollection of moving along the birth canal when being born: the well-known tunnel experience towards the light. Neurologists dispute the idea that the brain is capable of hanging on to pre-natal impressions as memories. But perhaps we are yet to discover the part of the brain that stores memories which are not a conceptual codification of experience.

It is understandable that, as with dreams, such impressionable near-death experiences demand explanation and interpretation. And just as with dreams it is natural to assume a soul detaching itself and drifting away from the body, viewing it from above (with what eyes?) and moving towards a divine light. (To verify whether this was a memory of one's own birth we would have to compare the near-death experiences of those born by Caesarean section with those who came into the world 'conventionally', and examine whether the Caesarean births had fantasies of *suddenly* being lifted up and it getting light in a similar situation.) The different way of remembering means that the process of dying begins with mental events which are also experienced as memories; in some people the process then turns into the tunnel experience, which is *not* experienced as a memory. This can be explained scientifically by the fact that totally different types of neuronal structures are active here from those associated with the *conceptual* understanding of experiences and known to us from other contexts in our lives as *memories*. In short, it might be that with the tunnel experience we are remembering for the first time in our life, now coming to an end, something that when we first experienced it we were *unable* to grasp conceptually, and thus when we remember it we cannot recognize it as a memory at all. And so we simply relive the emotional intensity of our birth.

If we see our life primarily as a stream of experiences and process of memory, death is the *cutting off* of this stream of experience. It is not implausible to assume that *before* our stream of experience is cut off, before our actual death, a total memory experience occurs for physiological reasons, as a sort of final feedback in the process of dying. This involves a recall of experiences that lie so far back that they have never entered our conscious mind before. Perhaps when the brain dies, areas of it are activated which lie so deep that in our normal waking state we have had no access to them or to the memories stored within them.

In a science-fiction film from 1968 (Kubrick's *2001: A Space Odyssey*) they switch off a computer with mental capacities comparable to those of a human being. As it is being turned off, one area of memory after another is deactivated and the computer loads increasingly basic programmes into its working memory until in the end it is singing children's songs. Might we not conceive of the death of our brain in the same way? Could it be that, while one mental skill after another disappears as we die, increasingly basic skills and experiences are activated as memories? Thus perceptions, feelings and thoughts from early childhood reappear until we arrive at the impressions of our birth. These we recall as a totally new and powerful tunnel-and-light experience, because up to the point of our birth we had never seen a tunnel or bright light, having existed solely in the darkness of the amniotic sac.

If this is the case – and from a scientific standpoint it is the most plausible way of looking at things – then we can expose the idea of a Day of Judgement, when our entire life is revealed, as a religious fantasy which accounts for the thrust of memories during the dying process. From a scientific perspective, all notions of a soul freeing itself from the body turn out to be a woolly explanation of the illusion produced by the dying person's body being fixed in one position for a long time. Thus the journey through the tunnel is not a crossing from this world into the next one, but a very elementary memory which we no longer recognize as such, a memory of our own birth, perhaps the earliest memory which we have preserved in our neuronal system as *our own*, and which can only be reactivated at this moment: when our brain fails from a lack of oxygen.

If we accept such a hypothetical explanation of the death experience relayed to us by some individuals who have been revived, then there is no reason to see dying as the end of this world and the beginning of the next, the birth of a new life we have to fear because we do not know what it has in store for us. Nor do we have to worry about how our soul, freed from our body, will cope with its new form of existence, because there is no longer any need to believe that this soul exists at all. On the contrary, the only reason for believing in the soul was to have an explanation for those experiences that can be traced back to unusual neuronal states when we are dying, which deviate sharply from our waking consciousness but also occur, in a somewhat more diluted form, in some flying dreams.

Why should we accept the scientific view rather than the religious one? Why should we reject the proposition that after death we journey into a divine realm of light, in favour of the notion that when we die we experience the slow decay of our mind? An epistemological argument for the scientific view comes from the philosopher David Hume. Let us say that someone claims to have had an experience which contravenes the laws of nature. What is the probability that this has actually happened? We will compare this probability with the probability that the person making the claim is a show-off trying to sound important. According to Hume the probability of the latter will always be higher than the former. This is how we should treat reports of near-death experiences, too. The probability that death and its aftermath are not subject to the known laws of nature is always lower than the probability that someone who has had such an experience will try to brag when talking about it, or that we *want* to believe them because the narrative satisfies our need for intensity.

Such a scientific view of dying may be less exciting, less emotionally intense than the idea of a soul that leaves the body at death and journeys into another world. In all likelihood, when the neurology of dying and death is complete it will be less interesting than the Tibetan or Egyptian Book of the Dead. After all, Christmas and Easter are less exciting without Santa Claus and the Easter Bunny. Moreover, this scientific view of dying also robs us of the solace that after death we somehow go on, that a bodiless consciousness continues to exist that nonetheless retains the memories of our physical existence. On the other hand, the scientific perspective not only eliminates the excitement and solace, but also the fear and terror accompanying many fantasies of hell – where there is no place for Santa and the Easter Bunny. We must not ignore the fact that, if we are not on the verge of dying, the idea of a supernatural continuation of our soul after death has something comforting about it, and stimulates an intensity of experience. This should make us suspicious of the idea in the first place. But we should also bear in mind that during the process of dying this notion can cause us extreme *disquiet*. Biologically speaking, the panic that arises during the process of dying vanishes when we have finally accepted that there is nothing else which can prevent our demise. It would be wrong, however, to let ourselves get upset by fairy tales dreamed up by know-alls and appropriated by ourselves because they are exciting or have comforted us at some point. The moment we get used to the idea that we are finite beings, we will also liberate ourselves from troubling fantasies in our final moments.

The final section of this paper will look at how we should deal with our need for intensity, which tempts us to stuff the repository of our beliefs with so many implausible claims.

Mathematics captures the individual

Dealing with our desires and the need for a greater intensity of experience requires us to recognize what our *individual* needs *really* are. Often we are unable to get them straight in our own minds because we are ashamed of them or we fail to detect them sufficiently in our actions, so that in some way we remain strangers even to ourselves. In order to cope successfully with our needs and desires we therefore have to *objectivize* them. Here, too, science promises great things in the future: it will allow us to measure how each of us is constituted vis-à-vis our needs. For *all* our needs are manifested in neuronal and hormonal states of excitement, and these are potentially measurable.

It is often claimed that science, which can measure and objectify, cannot capture the individual. But this idea is based on a deep-rooted and fundamental misunderstanding. Basically we know three different ways of accessing and representing reality: first the *narrative*, which says how something is, was or will be; second, the approach which *categorizes* or *classifies* things as *contrasts*, describing how light/dark, dry/wet, hot/cold, etc., they are, and uses these categories to explain the behaviour of an individual; and finally, the way of accessing and representing reality by means of *measuring* and by using mathematic scales and relationships. Let us call the first method of capturing reality the *Homeric* one and, following Kurt Lewin, the two others the *Aristotelian* and *Galilean* methods.

Because the individual, including the human individual, is still more complex and different than anything that can be encapsulated by general concepts, it has been argued that all we can do is *talk about* the individual in a more or less sketchy way. This view holds that the individual cannot be captured by the Aristotelian or Galilean approach. We should, therefore, adopt a Homeric approach to individuality, but not try to understand it theoretically. '*Individuum ist ineffabile*' ('The individual is ineffable') – this is a widespread misapprehension which stems from the reasoning outlined above. In fact, however, Lewin's finding (no longer a new one) is correct: measuring and representing attributes and relations using the language of mathematics makes individuality accessible. Building on the philosopher Ernst Cassirer's thesis that modern science has shifted from the concepts of essence and substance to measurement and the concept of function, Lewin writes: 'It is not the tendency towards the abstract, but the rejection of the abstract concept of category, the wish to record conceptually concrete individuality which is . . . the chief driving force behind the growth in quantification.' The Aristotelian method attempts to order individual entities into categories by labelling them as warm, dry, heavy, etc. Moreover, it aims to capture the *essence*, the *substance* of the individual. The Galilean method abandons both of these. Instead of ordering things directly into categories it measures calibrated attributes, meaning it is unnecessary to find an essence, as the identification of this essence is replaced by the representation of functional dependencies, which incorporate the calibrated attributes of an individual.

An example will illustrate this abstract issue. My brother and I both have a body mass. Let us say that, on a normal set of scales, we weigh 80 kilos. But if we measure our bodyweight with scientific precision we discover that there is a difference somewhere beyond the decimal point: I weigh 80.349 kilos, whereas my brother weighs 80.311. And if I explore the *development* of my and my brother's weight change, so long as I measure with sufficient accuracy, I will obtain different curves when charting weight over time.

If, on the other hand, I were to use the Aristotelian polarity of heavy and light, I would not be able to identify any difference. I would have to classify both of us as 'heavy' and say that our individuality could not be captured by our respective weights. If I were to select the Homeric approach – and describe that I had eaten this and that, whereas my brother had fed on that and this; that I had done this and that exercise and this and that work, whereas my brother had just slept – there would clearly be differences. But would they record the difference in weight? How should I attempt to *talk about* weight in the first place? After all, it is not a process or an event. At best I can talk about the actions, processes and events which resulted in my brother and me getting heavy. In the Homeric approach, too, it turns out that weight cannot be recorded as a measure of our individuality; indeed, it is not even a relevant factor here.

It is only in the measuring accuracy of the sciences that all measurable human attributes become potential criteria to distinguish one person from another. For the ability to register the difference in degree of an attribute between two different people, which makes it possible to distinguish between them as *individuals*, is only a question of measuring accuracy. In the courtroom, perfectly reconstructed fingerprints and DNA sequences are used to identify individuals. The Homeric approach, the narrative that describes who did what when, clearly plays a role here, too. But the scientific recording of the individual is the essential one.

The attributes of an individual which can be calibrated and measured are not a theoretical issue, but depend on the status of experimental and measuring research and the accuracy of the measuring instruments. Every person's desires and emotions are structured slightly differently. To be able to manage these prudently they need to get to know this structure as precisely as possible and eliminate all self-deception. Hardly anybody would admit to being timid or easily angered, and these categories – as Lewin established in his critique of non-measuring psychology – are not of much use in capturing an individual. If we describe one person as timid and the other as brave, what do we know *specifically* about the people concerned? Even if we introduce ratings from 1 to 10 we do not gain much. The appropriate metric objectification must, according to the Galilean method, involve *experiment with the individual* and *physiological assessment*. For example, a standard danger situation must be established to which individuals are exposed, and then the best possible measurements must be taken of the stress hormones they release and of the levels of their neuronal agitation in different parts of the brain.

If in this way we can come up with an objective and accurate psychogram of an individual, we can say without narrative inaccuracies and any self-deception how they are constituted as individuals in their needs and desires, just as today we are able to measure a person's cognitive abilities. Similar to the procedure in somatic medicine during blood sedimentation, which can provide information about many different physiological values, a quantitative psychogram about our tendencies towards fear and depression, joy and exuberance, our need for company and solitude, our sexual desire, our obsession with honour and fame, etc., could give an objective picture from the relevant tests. Our hormonal and neurological state in characteristic situations would be identified accurately and deliver the indicators of our actual state. The more accurately physiology and neurology measure our desires and emotions, the more accurately and objectively we can get to know ourselves.

Say that, in a frightening situation, a person P releases stress hormone X at the level 10.2, whereas another person Q produces the same hormone in the same situation, but only at the level 8.5. If, however, when X reaches 10 the aggression hormone Z is also produced, then P would know that they had a tendency towards a certain type of aggression in frightening situations. They could learn this without having to probe their unconscious and without having to rid themselves of their self-deceptions, an embarrassing process. Of course, for the technology to function the psychological terminology must be fine-tuned to the measuring process, so that we know *what* we are measuring and that there is no quibbling over words between the person being measured and the one doing the measuring, for example over what the terms 'fear' and 'aggression' mean. A consensual approach is needed to create a universal psychological terminology which eliminates conceptual differences. Although quibbling over the meaning of words is the business of philosophy, what matters here is that the person in question knows *what* aspect of them is being measured, so that the findings of the measuring process can properly allow them to recognize themselves more impartially. We can leave all discussions about the nature of fear and aggression to one side. Such debate belongs to the Aristotelian method. Here it is not about fear and aggression, but applying the methodological ideas outlined above to come up with calibrated attributes that make a specific person individual. There has to be agreement only between the measurer and the person being measured about the choice of words, but no need to try to understand the essence, which is in any case alien to the Galilean method.

What is more, the attributes measured and the concepts which describe them do not have to be organized into an overarching *general* psychological theory. It merely needs to be clear *why* when someone has *certain* feelings, *certain* hormonal and neuronal states are measurable. (One might also talk of psychological theories for individuals here.) If there is consensus over what is being measured, the person needs to learn to influence these states in *biofeedback processes*. People are able to influence their blood pressure, heartbeat, breathing if they can objectivize for themselves the corresponding attributes with measuring instruments. Once we have objectified the physiological and neuronal attributes which accompany certain desires and emotions, we need to construct the *apparatuses* which notify people of the relevant physiological values in their day-to-day lives.

The idea of such apparatuses is not new. As far back as 1928 the philosopher Rudolf Carnap, in relation to the problem of the knowability of other people's mental lives (the problem of so-called 'other minds'), wrote in his *Logischer Aufbau der Welt* (*The Logical Structure of the World*) about the setting up of what he called a 'brain mirror'. And even before Carnap there were ideas for the metric objectification of mental states, especially the graphic representation of ideas (using 'mind reading' on other people); for example, in 1885 the surgeon Eduard Albert's 'encephaloscope', or in 1896 the Parisian neurologist Hippolyte Baraduc's machine for producing 'psychoicons', 'pictures of the soul'. Today these dreams have already to a large extent become reality, and over the coming years the ability to represent people's neurological states will improve rapidly thanks to developments in nanotechnology and microcomputers.

Very soon it should be possible to plant nano-detectors in people's bloodstreams, which will be able to determine precisely the emergence and concentration trend of neurophysiologically relevant messenger substances in the organism, and then transmit this information to a microcomputer in the person's wristband, for example. The refining of magnet resonance procedures should make it possible in the foreseeable future to place detectors in a cap which identify patterns of agitation and excitement in the brain of the wearer and transmit these on to the same portable microcomputer. This can then combine brain data with data from the bloodstream and calculate the neurophysiological state of excitement at that moment. Like a permanent heart-rate monitor, permanent blood-pressure gauge or a permanent ECG worn by the individual, a 'neurophysiological mirror' or an 'emotiscope' needs to be developed which makes states relevant to desires and needs *precisely* readable, and in particular which *transmits* the information to an apparatus similar to a watch (such as: 'Aggression increasing sharply from 3 to 12 in the next 3 minutes' or 'Cheerfulness decreasing slowly from 8 to 6 in the next half an hour', etc.).

If we have learned the necessary biofeedback techniques by studying our neurophysiological mirror, we will be able to regulate actively our desires, needs and emotions in whichever direction we wish, depending on the tendencies we can identify on our emotiscope at that time. If, for any reason, we are *not* in a position to influence our feelings in a particular situation, perhaps because the level of excitement is already too high, we will still be able to opt for pharmacological regulation and take the appropriate boosters or blockers. These could also be available in small 'loadable' doses in the emotiscope, so that when the biofeedback failed a small injection into the pulse at the wrist could occur at the push of a button. It is also possible to imagine an emotiscope which would inject the appropriate chemicals automatically, whenever certain levels were exceeded, if surpassing these levels might have dangerous consequences for us or for others in our vicinity.

So, a person entering a dangerous situation could study their emotiscope to see whether the conditions that lead straight to aggression are already being measured, and then intervene in this physiological process in whichever way necessary with the appropriate auto-suggestion, for example by trying to master their rapidly developing fear.

This physiological/metric objectification would not only result in more accurate self-recognition, but also – if the appropriate auto-suggestion skills were acquired in biofeedback training

– bring about much *greater freedom and self-control.* Unlike a purely chemical control of emotions, which we know from psychopathology, here the person, *acting via their consciousness*, would be able to control themselves far more rapidly and accurately. Their self-reflection would merely be *supported* by the corresponding apparatuses, in the same way that we support our sense of time and schedule-related behaviour with watches.

Managing desires

These ideas are still utopian. But just as today leg or arm prostheses can be actively controlled after learning the necessary techniques, in the future we will be able to influence our physiology and neurology to a much greater extent than we already do naturally, for example by breathing faster or slower, or lying down and closing our eyes to relax. The metric monitoring of our physiology and neurology will be nothing more than an enhanced and more accurate self-*consciousness*; and auto-suggestion using the necessary equipment will be nothing more than an enhanced form of self-*control.* All we would then need would be something akin to a *dietetics of desire* tailored to each individual so that with this form of self-control we could learn how to avoid unhappiness and become happier. The following principles might be important when developing such a dietetics:

1. We should learn how to measure and control our emotional tendencies early in life, as a teenager. The earlier this learning process begins, the more skilful and flexible the later management of our moods will be.

2. We should live in professional and social environments which correspond to our emotional tendencies. Just as someone with little aptitude for maths or anything technical should not become a pilot, an individual with a tendency towards fear and excessive aggression should not become a soldier, because the poor match between their emotional tendencies and skills and the demands of the job would lead to unhappiness.

3. We should learn which emotional patterns represent a risk of becoming addicted, i.e., whether we have a propensity to develop a gambling or sex addiction, because addictions are one of the main sources of unhappiness.

4. We should cultivate social contact with people who are a good match according to our mood meter, i.e., we should live our private life in a social environment appropriate for us, because emotional dissonance in one's social life is a key source of unhappiness. (A neurophysiological 'matching' of people could be of great use here.)

5. Everybody must learn to 'restrict' the satisfaction of their desires and the occurrence of positive emotions. For these are all associated with 'costs' on the physiological side, as shown by the substance metric, which comes into play when desires and our satisfaction are involved. The satisfaction of desires and the production of pleasant feelings cannot be repeated as often as a person likes, as would be evident from the 'emotion mirror'.

In essence, these principles are merely an extension of what Plato describes in *The Republic*, when, in a simple metaphorical 'theory of elements or metals', he investigates people's characters according to the proportion of iron, silver and gold they contain, and allocates them a professional and social role which corresponds to their individual personality disposition or the 'alloy' of their soul. In our model this theory of elements is substituted by an accurate metric theory of substances, and the individual is given the opportunity to influence the composition of the substances which determine their situational moods. In psychopathology this control has been going on for years with chemicals. Just think of the prescription of fluotexine ('Prozac') as a stimulant and anti-depressive since the 1980s.

There is no need for a 'general theory of happiness' that goes beyond the five principles outlined above, because of the individual and metric nature of this emotional control. All that is needed is to establish the appropriate techniques (the emotion mirror) and learning practices (auto-suggestion skills) which allow every individual to objectivize their desires, needs and feelings, and to direct them in a way so that developments which cause unhappiness can be identified early and halted by the individuals themselves. *What* these developments that cause unhappiness are depends on the individual, for each person differs from every other in the degree of their desires and the rhythm of their emotional life.

Intensity and production of meaning in an enlightened existence

Desires, needs and emotions are *isolated* or *episodic* events, which, although they always recur in our lives, are not solely responsible for a person's happiness. Besides the satisfaction of desires and needs, and the intensity of positive feelings, the *relationship between a person's feelings and actions* plays a key role in judging whether our lives are happy or unhappy. This difference has also been characterized as that between 'feel-good happiness' and 'meaning'. We can also describe it as the need for *situational intensity* and *narrative coherence*. People might wish to have the most intense and positive feelings in individual situations, but they also want their life to have a *context* that can be reconstructed like a well-told story, rather than simply fragmenting into individual episodes.

If, for example, in a particular situation a person opts for the intensity of positive feelings which occurs with the satisfaction of sexual desire, the result might be the break-up of the family due to the jealousy this triggers in their partner. The family might not be merely a source of intensive and positive feelings, but, together with one's professional life, it usually provides a meaningful context. We do something in the present for our partner and especially our children so that something particular will happen in the future. These long-term perspectives often require sacrifices as far as situational emotional intensity is concerned. So someone in a position to experience the intensity of sexual pleasure with a new partner now not only has to weigh this pleasure up against the positive, intense feelings which their family affords them, because they are potentially putting the family structure at risk, but also weigh up the significance which the meaning of their family produces with this situational pleasure.

To avoid having to rate one's life as unhappy on the scale of meaning, it is crucial that the fourth principle set out above is met. For in unsatisfactory social relationships where there is a never-ending occurrence of situational emotional conflict, a person will readily sacrifice existing and future contexts of meaning to experience intense positive emotions again. There are important educational tasks here, too. People must learn to create contexts of meaning, in their careers by working in jobs that correspond to their skills; and in their social lives by learning to live with people with whom they can create an everyday context of meaning, rather than just moving in situational emotional conflicts and positive intensities.

Here, too, people must acknowledge their limits, i.e., learn to see their professional projects and private contexts of meaning as things which need to be shaped within their finite lives. Only if we succeed in this will death no longer appear as the destruction of something which 'had not even started yet'. Although we may not fear death because we do not see the agonies of hell or other alien terrors before our eyes, the feeling that we have not yet accomplished anything meaningful may produce a fear of death. For this reason, within the context of an enlightened education we need to accept the finitude of our own existence before we can properly schedule contexts of meaning. Those who fail to take into account their finite lifetime might well make a poor assessment of how long it takes to create contexts of meaning. At first they underestimate the lack of these contexts, then finally, at death's door, find such a lack terribly painful.

It has been argued that time is the 'substance' from which humans 'exist' as subjects. Just as people must learn to control the intensity of their situational, emotional lives to avoid unhappiness, they likewise must learn to treat their finite lifetime as a resource for producing meaning. The happiness of enlightened people will consist neither in a permanent state of pleasure, nor in a quest for salvation in the world to come, but will be a result of the skill of avoiding situational unhappiness which comes from striving for intense feelings, and to learn to produce meaning which is compatible with intensity in the finite lifetime available to us all. In view of increasing life expectancy as a result of medical progress, an important second skill is the ability to create ever more meaningful contexts within a finite period of time. A prerequisite of this skill is to have a view on one's own finitude which is without fear. This can only be acquired in an enlightened culture and a corresponding education system. Besides the quest for scientific and technological progress, therefore, of key importance is the refining of an education system which is fully committed to truth and which has eliminated all susceptibility to superstition and self-deception. People who have at their fingertips the scientific and technological opportunities to gain objective self-awareness, and who have learned to control themselves in an unprejudiced way will also be able to avoid unhappiness.

Erwin Weinberger
Cambridge, Massachusetts

CHAPTER THREE

The happiness of peace of mind

The changeability of people

Not everybody can be happy as they are. But it is a misconception to believe that people are fixed as they are and that the *world* needs to be changed so they can be happy in a world tailored to their needs. People are very different and to cater for some of these differences it may make sense to create alternatives in the world. If there are both steps and ramps at the entrance to a building, allowing wheelchair users to access it as well as those who can walk, this is a sensible arrangement. But not all instances of human difference are like this. If one person is addicted to alcohol, another to gambling, a third to heroin, happiness is not achieved by giving the first as much alcohol as possible, the second as much money as they need to gamble and the third as much heroin as they want. It would be wrong to *adapt* the world to addictions rather than trying to *free* people from their addictions. In our second example we would consider *changing people* to be the right course of action rather than modifying the world. And if we could possibly cure disabled and paralysed people in wheelchairs of their disabilities and paralyses, this solution would be preferable to building ramps.

The fact that people can change, that able-bodied people can be paralysed by an accident, that angry people can change into sympathetic ones, peaceful types into aggressive individuals, addictive people into sober-minded ones – all this proves the flexibility and malleability of human nature. Human nature is as malleable as the outside world, more malleable in many respects. In our culture, however, we have become used to blaming the world for our misfortunes, and thus we want to change it rather than thinking about how we have developed *ourselves* and whether this development *on our part* has led to a character which is incompatible with happiness, no matter what we undertake in the world.

While people are young we acknowledge that they are changeable. For to educate someone is to change them. There is a variety of aims in education. But only seldom do educators seem to think about influencing and changing their pupils so that they can be happy. Usually the focus is on teaching specific cultural techniques which make pupils tolerable members of the society in which they are raised, i.e., instructing them in cleanliness and table manners. After that it is about learning skills which have the potential to improve one's chances of obtaining goods and status, such as reading, writing, arithmetic and other training. Finally people need to learn how to use machines such as cars and computers. And yet it is uncertain whether these things actually contribute to our happiness. In spite of having had a solid education as children and adolescents, many people are unhappy as adults. This seems always to have been the case. Otherwise it is hard to explain why schools of philosophy in Europe and centres of wisdom in Asia have existed for thousands of years, where *adults* have been taught how to escape their unhappiness. The fact that there has been and still is this 'education of grown-ups' (as Stanley Cavell puts it in response to Wittgenstein) shows that some teachers believe that older people are changeable, too. The teachings which have been developed for the education of adults are ancient.

For this reason everything there is to know about happiness has already been known for years. Since Epictetus and Spinoza or since Buddha and Jesus people have been able to know, assuming they *wanted* to, how to attain happiness. This is because for many thousands of years people have been examining themselves, their experiences of their own feelings, actions and thoughts, and how these relate to happiness, even though for some curious reason the education of children has hardly touched on this aim. Because people have long had success in this process of self-inquiry, nobody need wait for future advances in science to be liberated from their unhappiness. For scientific progress chiefly relates to human understanding of the laws of the *outside world* and the possibility of changing this outside world. The idea that other people could liberate us from our unhappiness by making some discovery about the world and how to improve it, is the most fundamental error in the debate over whether people can be happy and, if so, how. In what follows I shall endeavour to avoid this basic error.

The fact that there is a tradition of teaching people to be happy which dates back millennia does not mean that the path to happiness lies primarily in studying this tradition. Engaging with the tradition will not do any harm up to a certain point, but it is not a self-education to happiness. In many cases this sort of research is more a *surrogate* for an incomplete education to happiness, which substitutes scholarship for such an education. Just as nobody will ever become a good cook or have a full stomach by poring over a cookbook, nobody will become happy by studying texts. We need more than that. In this paper, therefore, I cannot outline and interpret the writings about the teachings of Jesus or Buddha, or discourses on and by Epictetus and Spinoza. Even though these writings do play a part in my investigation, this essay can only be an attempt to answer the question of whether human happiness is possible and, if so, how; not a scholarly study of certain writings. Rather, I have put together some very general views from different teachings, without designating one particular tradition as 'the right one' or 'the original'. This paper does not focus on arguments between schools of thought or proofs of precedence, which would only be a distraction from the question of happiness. Happiness has nothing to do with being right or being the first. References to so-called 'classical' texts are thus merely suggestions for those who would like to read around the topic more widely. There is no intention here of claiming any authoritative interpretation of this or that point in this or that text.

Wealth

It has long been known that people can be happy if they achieve *peace of mind*. By peace of mind we mean that people lose their worries – temporarily, at least – live wholly in the present and focus their full attention on what is happening now. The only path to happiness or peace of mind is that created by *our own efforts*. We must make efforts not to be distracted from the present, not to pursue goals which cause us worries, not to forget that our own powers are limited, that the ideas of the good life that we grow up with are usually mistaken and that we must free ourselves from them. Thanks to popular misconceptions people allow themselves to be educated by other people into all manner of dependencies. But those who wish to be happy must strive to liberate themselves from such dependencies. As Spinoza, in response to the Stoics, had already concluded in his *Tractatus de Intellectus Emendatione*, the chief misconceptions are to believe that *wealth*, *status* and *pleasure* make us happy. It may seem somewhat simplistic and trite to examine these misconceptions, seeing that everybody is aware of them already, either as a result of their own experiences or from hearsay – they have been known for millennia. I shall afford them brief consideration nonetheless, and it is important that they are presented as plainly as possible to avoid them being seen as 'Buddhist views' or 'Christian views' or 'Stoic views'. In this way they will not appear as representative of any particular school we might enter an argument with, but as basic, general principles that we need not argue against and which we can appreciate, whether we are Buddhists, Christians, Stoics or anything else for that matter. Because even arguments between different schools are distractions from our focus on the search for happiness.

That people make such errors in the first place is due to the fact that their education in childhood and adolescence did *not* focus on their happiness, or that their teachers did not know themselves what it is to lead a happy life. The first change that most people experience in education, therefore, is to become beings who pursue goals that make them *unhappy*. The majority of people's early education is an education towards unhappiness. For this reason the education of adults is usually a *re-education* in which people learn to rid themselves of the goals they developed as children and adolescents. Traditionally this process is also known as de-education (in contrast to education).

Because people in most Western societies believe that *wealth* makes us happy, the overwhelming majority of them, succumbing to the *first* misconception, spend a lifetime striving for wealth: accumulating resources which are totally unnecessary for their own survival and which are not used for the survival of others, either. If a person living alone bought ten litres of milk and ten loaves of bread every day, we would regard this as irrational behaviour. Yet apparently, the existence of money has made the accumulation of resources exceeding what is needed for survival somehow less irrational. For unlike milk and bread, money cannot deteriorate – it represents the potential to acquire things which keep us alive.

In wealthy societies people are either busy taking money off other people, making themselves richer in the process, or acquiring things that supposedly satisfy needs which have nothing to do with survival, but are created by the emotions of ambition and envy. It is known that these secondary and tertiary needs for certain things, produced by our emotions, are connected to the symbolic social value of goods. Brands of certain cars or clothes, for example, signal the group to which the owner with a particular status belongs within a social hierarchy. People are taught the need to want to signal to others that they are assertive competitors, stylistically confident aficionados, seductive lovers, intellectuals independent of the market, etc. Brand advertising creates the association between objects and these social signals and tries, using processes of conditioning, to consolidate these associations in people's minds. If this works the objects are not bought for their utility value alone, but for their symbolic social value.

While manufacturers are able to invent all manner of ideals of group identity and self-expression, and fabricate the need to belong and to mark oneself out from others, they can sell many more goods than pure survival would require. The needs that the utility value of goods satisfies are very rapidly exhausted, whereas the needs which result from social comparison and its related emotions seem to be almost inexhaustible. For this reason the opportunity of earning money with the symbolic social value of goods is obviously much greater than that of getting rich through their utility value. If everybody has a shirt and nobody is cold anymore, then you need to produce a brand of shirt for laid-back people, one for orderly people, one for those motivated by sex, one for easy-going older people, and then sell the different shirts to those who want to belong to the corresponding group. When everybody's thirst is quenched, you need to find or create one water for the health-conscious and one for environmental activists, one beer for football fans and one for the style-conscious manager, a wine for distinguished urban intellectuals and one for those who love the simple country life, and then find or create the group of people who apply the relevant descriptions to themselves, who want to obtain an 'identity', as it is also called, by acquiring such goods. In this way society is divided into groups of the same sex, the same talent, the same body size, the same age and similar professions, etc., which in the imagination produce further groups and ideals of group identity that are symbolically represented by goods. You cannot sell much to someone who only sees themselves as a person who needs to eat, drink, clothe themselves and put a roof over their head; whereas somebody who wants to signal to others that they are a strong man, an intelligent person, a sporty type or a lover of northern climes, etc., can be sold much more.

In wealthy societies a key element of a child's upbringing is promoting the ambition to earn money. This is done by impressing on the child the idea that one day they will have to earn themselves and, through the messages of advertising, bringing them up to be consumers who can parade as something in particular. Thus at a very early age the child is taught to aspire to an abstract potential such as money, and to develop the secondary and tertiary needs to mark oneself out and belong, which might be symbolized by a particular brand of clothes, for example. This is the teaching of capitalist societies. Advertising messages exert influence over the imagination and ideas of children just as churches and schools do. This influence is only seldom regarded to be part of a child's education, however. For people to be good consumers they must remain under age as adults, too, and allow themselves to be persuaded independently of their weakened self-awareness that they have certain needs to belong and stand out and that they are lacking a certain product essential to their happiness. Grown-ups, too, must see their social identity as something which is fashioned chiefly by the acquisition of goods and not by the relations of friendship, kinship and collegiality. Besides physical and emotional survival, the survival of a wide-ranging *social* identity emerges, an identity which is only fabricated in a wealthy society.

In societies that aspire to wealth, therefore, adults essentially fall into two groups: one which wants to *take* the money that others earn by inventing fairy tales about supposed needs and the importance of certain goods, and which aims to keep other people at the level of children so that their fairy tales are believed; and those who allow their money to be taken because needs are aroused and goods are sold that supposedly satisfy these needs.

Both groups are mistaken over what makes a happy life.

This is primarily a result of the fact that the accumulation of money rather than the satisfaction of needs is the ultimate goal in the most advanced wealthy societies. Although money was originally a *means* for human relationships in which goods were exchanged that satisfied needs, later on, as Karl Marx recognized, the needs and the exchange became the means of getting more money, and getting more money became an *end in itself*. So what happens, as often in unhappy relationships, is a reversal of the *means–end relationship*. Money, as an *abstract* wealth, as merely a potential for satisfying needs, represents the *actual* goal of action (insofar as we can still talk of 'action' here), a goal not consciously chosen by anybody. This results in a peculiar 'alienation', as Marx calls it, of the relations of people to each other and of their relations to things, 'the relationship itself between things, man's operation with them, becomes an operation of an entity outside man [money]* and above man'. So those who have a lot of money as well as those who have little are equally *victims of the structure* of capitalist economic activity to make more money, in which human needs are still only secondary means of increasing wealth.

The human need to develop and realize long-term *life plans*, which (also mistakenly) are seen as a requirement for happiness, represents an obstacle to increasing wealth in today's rich societies. This is further evidence that human happiness is not an objective of processes in wealthy societies. These societies tend, therefore, to criticize as 'conservative' and 'obstinate' people with firm ideas and values by which they try to lead their lives, because they 'do not

---

* My brackets.

move with the times'. In such societies changeability and change are publicized as *values in themselves*, which require no further justification. If the burden of justification is successfully shifted onto those who have no desire to change their circumstances, whereas those who do change are liberated from having to justify their actions, we are left only with people who – depending on how the market develops – do, wish and think something different, irrespective of what 'the market' 'recommends'. Because markets change ever more rapidly, allowing wealth to be increased ever more rapidly; people in modern wealthy societies are forever having to alter their needs and identities and, in particular, divide up their time in such a way that makes it impossible to realize their life's plans. However, the basic realization that striving for wealth does not make people happy, independent of the reinterpretation of earning money from a means to an end, is much older than capitalism and Marx's analysis of it. We already find it in ancient Europe, in the work of Aristotle, for example.

This error of capitalism makes unhappy those who become rich, as well as those whom the rich try to keep immature (in the sense of preventing independent thought about one's own needs and social identity) and exploit in order to get rich. For those who strive for wealth have to do it with great intensity; they need constantly to develop new strategies of earning money and must not waste time honing the ability – which in theory they possess like everybody else – to experience the present. If they are in possession of the wealth they have aspired to, they no longer have anything to strive for, but nor are they in a position to experience the present, which is why their life comes across as empty and meaningless. They become just as unhappy, albeit in a different way, as those they have led by the nose, appropriating their money by selling them goods useless for their survival, or persuading them of social needs which have generated the demand for such goods. When consumers reach a certain age, they tend to wonder why they are working for all these goods and why one need seems to follow another in their life.

Viewed from the outside, there is something absurd about a life focused on wealth, because in it the circulation of something dead, money, seems to determine the development of something living, human existence. It is as if the people in these societies had stepped into a machine which has nothing to do with their happiness, but to which they have to adapt their needs and entire rhythm of life in order to stay alive.

Moreover, in a society labouring under this delusion goods need to be produced continually and in vast quantities, so they can then be sold to those kept immature in order to appropriate their money. As has long been known, this mass production, which is necessary if you wish to sell something to a large number of people, harms the so-called natural basis of human (but not just human) life. Damaging and ultimately destroying the natural basis of life also makes people unhappy, because it brings us into an unhealthy competition, not only for natural resources such as oil, coal, gas, etc., but also for elemental goods such as clean air, clean water and uncontaminated soil, giving rise to the fear that soon there will no longer be a basis for life on earth, neither for us, nor our descendants. If, as Aristotle did, we see the fundamental task of politics as providing clean air and clean drinking water, then capitalist economic activity impedes the completion of these most basic political tasks. Put another way, politics has to focus constantly on compensating for the damage caused by such activity.

The reason why this economic system and the way of life that accompanies it has not been abandoned, however, is because the aspiration for wealth is *addictive*, and because in these societies there are scarcely any institutions encouraging the necessary de-education processes to free people from this addiction. Initially, alcohol can be a substance for relaxation, and cocaine one for stimulation, but a sudden change from using these substances recreationally to becoming addicted means that the enjoyment of them becomes an end in itself, so that people work and relax in order to obtain alcohol and cocaine, but not the other way round. Likewise, in a culture which has entered the 'stage of addiction' of a wealthy society, the accumulation of capital becomes an end in itself to which all else is subordinated. This is why people in these societies, even though they are unhappy, regard the quest for wealth and goods as the *right goal* of their lives, for which one has to *accept* the obstruction of elementary political tasks. Even in democratic societies, therefore, no political parties are elected which would bring capitalism to an end. For people are afraid of losing their jobs and thus the source of their income or their wealth. Without work or the ability to acquire goods they would have no idea what to do, even if their food and lodging were provided, because they have not learned how to experience the present, or they have lost this faculty.

Power and status

The *second* misconception which Spinoza outlines (also as a response to the Stoics in the treatise cited above) is the idea that achieving *power* and *status* will lead to a happy life. Because people believe that power and status make us happy they aspire to high office and influence. In order to attain these positions and influence they have to use other people who can help them along the path, but who cannot secure these positions themselves, because, after all, power and status are scarce resources, like money. In the worst case this exploitation of other people includes military service.

Anybody who strives for power and status as means to happiness, exploiting others to achieve their aspirations, but preventing these from enjoying the ever scarcer resources of power and status themselves, cannot help but *deceive* other people, making them promises which ultimately cannot be kept. This obligation to deceive gives rise to unhappiness. For nobody chooses to associate with liars in the long run. What is more, such a person must be extremely tenacious in their pursuit, for they will face an unremitting challenge from others for the scarce resources of power and status. In fact, the competition for office and status is a permanent *battle*. Those involved in the battle must, therefore, think constantly about their *future* objectives and cannot bother themselves with the present, because anybody in the thick of a battle must be 'proactive', predicting their opponent's moves. The pursuit of power and status, therefore, leads to a life which is not dissimilar to a state of war – Thomas Hobbes described this as the natural condition of man: an existence which is 'solitary, poor, nasty, brutish and short', although this does an injustice to many animal lives which are probably far more noble, that is to say more oriented to the present, than people usually believe.

Once those striving for the goals of power and status have attained them, they will realize that these goods have not made them happy but lonely, and thus they will be unhappy at having *squandered* their life on such a pursuit. For solitude is only unproblematic for those people who have learned to experience the present and who have peace of mind, free from anxiety. Solitude makes most other people unsettled and worried, because they no longer have anybody to confirm their social identity or who might help them in a potential emergency. Usually, therefore, solitude leads to abstract worries, sometimes even fear and panic. Those who lack peace of mind are especially overcome by such fear and panic during the process of dying, because this process, too, is one of isolation. After all, we die alone, for ourselves: death separates us from all other people. People who cannot take a simple view of the process of death when it is happening, but who try as usual to think of the future, are in a terrible situation, because they no longer have a future. The attempt to direct one's mind and efforts to the future, something which no longer exists for this dying mind, is a hopeless undertaking. For this reason death is catastrophic for those who strive for power and status. They need to picture themselves as immortal, as endlessly powerful. We can see this from the fact that many old men still wage a bitter struggle for power and status.

The person who strives for status and power will have not only made themselves unhappy through their endeavours, but also many other people who will have been deceived or forcibly pushed aside to prevent their occupying the spot that the person has claimed for themselves; for it is in the very nature of power and status that not *everybody* can live with a full ration of them. Power is power *over* others, and status is status *above* others. Power and status can only have value, i.e., be goods, where the powerless and those without status exist. Like money, power and status cannot be shared out at will. It is true of all scarce goods that the pursuit of them inevitably leads to conflict. In this respect, therefore, we can see that striving to achieve an awareness of the present is a profoundly different good. Everybody has their present at every moment; it cannot be taken away from them. Awareness of the present is something which can be shared out at will without decreasing. Awareness of the present is thus a good which is not scarce and for which there can be no competition.

Once someone has attained power and status that person must live with the permanent fear that those they have pushed aside through deceit will seek revenge, join forces and turn against them. Thomas Hobbes elaborated this idea, too. The possession of power, therefore, is necessarily tied up with the fear of losing it again. It is known, however, that constant fear is another feeling which makes people unhappy. Particularly striking in Shakespeare's plays is the depiction of the unhappiness of the pursuit and possession of power. The emotions linked to the quest for power and fame and which determine this sort of unhappy life are *ambition* and *vanity*. Ubiquitous in many modern communities, they are almost typical of people belonging to the so-called upper classes of these societies. The following quotation is an accurate critique of these emotions: 'We can say that ambition and vanity are the key driving forces in human society. This desire for fame is an exaggeration, a tumour that never stops growing. In this ever-moving crescendo people lose the principle of sticking with something, a principle which alone could give us the common sense to put a stop to this frenetic action before the final explosion. Vanity, therefore, is a conquering will of the ego which desires ever more, and which in its imperialism strives to occupy as much space as possible.'

In the life which strives for power and fame there literally needs to be an increase, both spatially and temporally, in the extent or 'span' of the ego: the political realm which is ruled; the microphone, which extends the acoustic area 'possessed' by the person concerned; the large print run, which supposedly increases the concentrated attention given to their own utterances; the many children that will survive them, possibly continuing what they have started and who will think of them, etc. All this leads to unhappiness, too, because what death destroys is forever getting bigger, because what needs to be *protected* is getting more and more complex. Over the course of time a life which expands in this way cannot but pay less and less attention to the present, whereas more and more means are expended on fostering, protecting and preserving the expansion of the 'I'.

Pleasure

Finally, because people believe that *pleasure* makes them happy they seek out pleasurable sensations. But the short-term, ephemeral sensations of pleasure that result from delicious food, sex and taking euphoria-inducing drugs lead to the sensory organs becoming accustomed to them. What was wonderful the first time becomes boring on the hundredth occasion. Occasionally, we must also develop a sensibility for the stimuli that cause pleasure, so that something which is fairly pleasant first time around induces euphoria the third time. We become accustomed to these pleasures, too, which means that the intensity of the stimuli or the dose of the substances causing pleasure needs to be increased. This increase in the intensity of the stimuli has to occur on a continual basis if the sensations of pleasure are to be repeated. If it is not possible to repeat the sensations of pleasure, this gives rise to displeasure and cravings. Because the sources of pleasure, whether they be sexual, culinary or of any other type, are linked to the *expenditure of money*, the compulsion to increase the intensity of the stimuli brings with it the compulsion to earn more money necessary for the acquisition of ever more expensive means of pleasure. With respect to socially outlawed substances such as heroin or cocaine, we speak of 'drug-related crime'. But the usual forms of money-earning, which allow us to afford alcohol, cigarettes and contact with sexual partners we tolerate for a while, follow the same pattern. There is only a slight, rather than fundamental difference between the despondency of drug-related crime and that of the life society does not outlaw. In addition, therefore, to the desire for things that give us pleasure and the worry that we might not acquire them, there is also the desire for money and the worry that we might not get that either. It is only in the moments of pleasure, which generally become ever shorter, that we are freed from this dependency on the means of pleasure and the means to acquire these means of pleasure. Rather than pursuing happiness, this way of life strives to produce feelings of pleasure as feelings of happiness, or to acquire the means to produce them.

In one sense, short-term pleasures can be described as *vague reflections* of happiness. For they lead at least to a momentary concentration on the present. But as with intense pain they do this through the *intensity* of the sensation. It is the strength of the sensory impression rather than the will of the observer which forces us to focus our attention on it. For, of course, very few people want to feel pain, but they do have to focus their attention on the pain if it kicks in with a certain intensity. The ability to focus one's attention on the present is not trained by intense feelings (the opposite, in fact). Rather, feelings of pleasure and pain are followed by *actions* geared to the future, if the pleasurable circumstances are to be *repeated* or the painful ones *avoided* by these actions. People who pursue pleasure in this way, moreover, often feel less intense sensations to be banal and irrelevant.

Furthermore, once a certain level of intensity has been reached, the stimuli which induce pleasure damage the organism that senses pleasure. Those people, therefore, who believe that pleasure makes us happy not only bring displeasure on themselves when the provider of pleasure is absent; at some point they also tend to suffer physically from the destruction of their sensory organs, which can no longer keep up with the ever increasing intensity of the stimuli. All this was already known in antiquity by Epictetus, and the unhappiness of a life which is on a constant quest for more intense sensations of pleasure, and in which the stimuli continually have to be intensified, has been portrayed in many novels, recently by Michel Houllebecq, for example.

Although all these views are ancient and can be read about in countless books, the number of people who fall victim to these *delusions* continues to be extraordinarily high; indeed, whole societies are still structured in a way that their members are almost destined for unhappiness via these delusions. Frequently people fall victim to two or all three of the delusions and strive for wealth, power, status and pleasure all at the same time. The different tendencies of pursuing these goods are also linked sometimes, because with money you can obtain power and status as well as pleasure. Capitalist societies, therefore, are not just propagators of the wealth delusion, but of the power and pleasure delusions, too.

It still appears to be the case that only by *isolating* ourselves from the societies that exist, by taking on the role of the *misfit*, we might be able to distance ourselves from these delusions so that they do not determine our lives, and thus be in a position to free ourselves from them. It is extremely unusual to find individuals who keep their distance from these objectives from the outset and who reject any involvement in the societies concerned. If we do not belong to this rare group of people, however, most of us need a teacher for adults who can support us in our endeavour to liberate ourselves from such delusions, and a strong determination to take seriously the wish for a happy life and to use the rest of our lives for making this wish come true, rather than for anything else. At the end of Beckett's *Waiting for Godot* Vladimir says to Estragon, 'Well, shall we go?' Estragon replies, 'Yes, let's go,' but neither of them moves. Maybe that is how people relate to these ancient ideas. Instead of taking them seriously and abstaining from the pursuit of life goals which make us unhappy, in most countries dominated by European and North American culture the strategy is to improve life by means of technological progress based on scientific knowledge, and otherwise to leave people alone with their delusions. For, in fact, the delusions are not recognized as such; instead the belief goes that we only need to increase the general wealth so that *everybody* is rich, extend the possibilities for fame so that *everybody* can enter the public arena, multiply the sources of pleasure so that *everybody* can enjoy them, and improve medicine so that *everybody* can be cured of the consequences of their intense pleasure. From this perspective happiness is not a problem of the right objectives in life, but a technical problem of the right economic activity, the right media structure, a repressed morality of pleasure which can be changed socially and technologically, and of progress in medicine. In truth, however, without a change in our life goals, all of this will merely lead to a technological acceleration of the pursuit of money, power and pleasure, and thus to unhappiness, something we can actually see with our own eyes.

Maybe it is a biologically conditioned *laziness* which makes people stick with the inclinations they have become accustomed to follow, even when their survival is no longer threatened. Maybe the pursuit of power, money and pleasure represents a continuation of modes of behaviour which originate in the biological struggle for survival: as natural beings people had to learn to dominate nature and their enemies, i.e., gain power, gather resources and reproduce to preserve themselves as individuals and as a species, the success of which was indicated by pleasure. In this respect, the major error of the pursuit of pleasure would be the inclination to persist with the genetically determined struggle to preserve the individual and the species in circumstances where the survival of the individual and the species had long been secured, but where continuing to strive for the accumulation of resources and maximization of pleasure might even *endanger* this survival. The fact that our biological survival is not dependent on our striving for happiness could mean that the pursuit of true happiness (rather than the sham happiness of the 'exaggerated' struggle for survival) is not supported by a 'biological programme' which would be the product of natural evolution.

Just as truth is not necessarily a requirement for biological survival, as Nietzsche realized, and maybe delusion furthers life much more, happiness is far less a requirement of a successful *biological* existence than unhappiness. Maybe this is why so many efforts to attain true happiness appear so painstaking. For it is difficult to work against something which our own biology favours. In fact, the pursuit of the happiness represented by peace of mind is far less costly in terms of our own energy expenditure than the pursuit of power, money or pleasure, the boundlessness of which ultimately wears down the person endeavouring to attain them. It is truly astonishing that the biological and physical sciences have failed to accept the discrepancy between striving for survival and striving for happiness.

The universality of suffering

One reason for the absence of reasoned thinking about the relationship between survival and the pursuit of happiness could be that '*suffering*' is not a scientific concept. At most, science recognizes the physiologically measurable counterpart of *pain*. Although biology and many philosophies which reflect it look at organic life as a process of problem-solving, they focus on the problems of *survival* and *reproduction*. Living beings that solve these problems have not solved the problem of suffering, however. For suffering is not a problem that can be solved in life; rather it is a problem of life itself, which can only be solved 'definitively' when life *ceases*. 'There is . . . a total contradiction in wanting to live life without suffering, which can also be found in the oft-used term "blessed life".' A *reduction* in suffering, which in an ideal scenario leads to peace of mind, and which represents the only happiness attainable in life, is possible only where people realize that it is not completely down to us how full of suffering a life proves to be for the being living it. For all living things are finite and have finite power. Every finite being can be overpowered or dominated by one or several others. And such processes necessarily involve suffering.

Peace of mind or happiness that is humanly possible depends on an understanding of the limited power we have to shape our own lives. We therefore need to acknowledge the *malleability of our own nature*, as well as its *finitude* if we are to come close to a happiness that is humanly possible or peace of mind. For only this understanding will liberate us from the idea that suffering indicates an *error* committed on our part, that suffering signals a *technical problem* we have not yet solved or even a *punishment* for some guilt we have burdened ourselves with. None of this is true. Avoiding all errors, solving all of life's problems, avoiding all guilt does not free anyone from suffering. For everyone enters this finite existence unasked, without choice, and with limited power, and everyone must exit life again through the process of dying, which is always accompanied by a degree of suffering. Suffering is a necessary aspect of the finitude of life and not the result of having led the wrong life. The wrong life, on the other hand, in which peace of mind is *impossible*, is the result of the illusion that suffering can be avoided, or of the omnipotence behind the idea that the world can be changed in whichever way we want until it assumes a form in which everybody, despite their diversity, can be happy.

It has long been known in both Western and Eastern philosophy and science that there are no individual, solitary facts that can be viewed in isolation as *real* facts in themselves. Each individual thing is real because it has particular effects and because other things have an effect on it. In the East this view was advanced by Buddha and his followers; in the West by the process philosophers from Heraclitus to Whitehead. The principal effects of the facts which we feel, perceive or think are either repellent or attractive; i.e., what we feel, perceive or register we either *never* want to feel, perceive or register again or we want to feel, perceive or register them *over and over again*. It is almost impossible to come into contact with facts *without* feeling emotions of displeasure and pleasure, and thus entering a mindset of flight or pursuit. This wider understanding of the link between contact with the world and emotionally conditioned endeavour has been around longer in the East than the West (in the East it goes back to Buddha; in the West we find it in the work of Epicurus and Spinoza). One aspect of the reality of all the things which exist for us, therefore, is the fact that we feel either pleasure or pain when we come into contact with them. Sometimes this feeling is so marginal that we do not even notice; at other times it is so strong that we enter a state of ecstasy or despair, or we die.

Suffering occurs when this contact and the emotionally conditioned endeavour which accompanies it lead to *habits* that result in a particular form of life, full of suffering, which mainly consists of a permanent oscillation between avoiding and seeking. This form of life has also been categorized and described as *unfree*. The quest for happiness focuses on putting an end to this unfreedom.

Who is happy?

The fact that people struggle for survival and happiness, that they feel pleasure and pain, that they suffer and try to avoid suffering, begs the question as to *who* is actually suffering here? Who is struggling to survive and find happiness? The false assumption is often made that either an 'I' or a subject or the capacity for reflection must be there from the start of human existence as something *pre-determined* and *absolute*, or that these entities *do not exist at all*, that they are an illusion. This is a false set of alternatives. If, like Buddha, Heraclitus or Whitehead, you acknowledge the process by which everything that is real comes into being and exists in relation to other real things, and when the conditions of its coming into being and preservation no longer exist it disappears again – i.e., there are no absolutes in this world, only things that are contingent, conditional – you must also accept that the entities of the I, the self or subjectivity come into being and survive under certain conditions, and when these conditions disappear they vanish again. Without the development of sensory organs, hormonal systems and nerve centres it is clear that no aspirations and perceptions would come into being. The fact that when these systems break down the corresponding mental processes fail or, as we have become used to saying, are 'disturbed', shows that the material complexity described by physiologists and the mental complexity that we experience are one and the same. It can exist in different ways depending on whether we merely observe and describe such a system or whether we actually *are* it, too.

Once a relatively complex nervous and sensory system is present, this system can also be influenced by gestures, language and all other forms of influence that exist in society. A small child that is able to perceive sensations and seek food is subject to the praise and chastisement of its parents and language. The child changes as a result of these, just as it changes as a result of the food it eats and the movements it makes. It grows, learns to walk, thereby effecting changes in its brain, copies gestures and facial expressions, and finally the language of other people. Once more we can ask *who* is growing here, learning to walk, effecting changes in its brain, copying gestures and facial expressions and finally learning to use language? The answer is that this is *a different* system at each stage of development, a changing material and mental complex which only achieves unity in the context of its development, in which one thing results from another. The child that cannot walk yet and cannot focus its eyes on the objects around it is a different being from that which can do these things. And the system which can walk and copy but which cannot yet talk is different again from that which can take part – understanding and speaking – in the linguistic exchanges in its environment. The person who can no longer walk because they have become too weak for it in old age is another being. And the person who no longer knows what is going on around them, and finally stops talking, is yet another. It is important to recognize that in this process between genesis, being born, living, dying and decomposing, an array of material and mental complexes appear and disappear, which are described only very inadequately by the concepts I, self and subject. The being that strives to preserve its complexity emerges already in its mother's womb and only disappears with the process we call dying. The being that perceives external things, focusing its attention on them, does not appear until outside its mother's womb and can vanish again prior to the state we call death (in deep unconsciousness, for example, where certain efforts to stay alive are still functioning). In between these two states, through human development processes, a being appears which can talk and say 'I'.

The development process which is a result of other people's influence, especially the influence of language, is of particular interest because through our actions we intentionally produce something in other people, whereas prior to this something occurs which is independent of human intention (although fundamentally dependent). During a child's upbringing it does this or that and is praised by its parents for the one thing and chastised for the other. This process of praise and censure is accompanied by displays of affection and utterances such as 'Johnny did that very well' or 'Johnny must never do that again' and the corresponding physical chastisement. The child then develops an association between the memory of what it has just done, the word 'Johnny' and the pleasant or unpleasant feelings which are bound up with praise or censure. In this way, besides developing the propensity to do one thing rather than another, the child learns the idea that it is the *protagonist*, the *agent*, the one *responsible* for its deeds. The feelings of pride and humiliation which are tied up with praise and censure produce the idea of the acting subject or agent in those who are praised or censured, as David Hume realized.

The notion of the acting subject, therefore, is *produced* in the social process of education, albeit as a side-effect of those doing the teaching. The latter aim to teach children to do one thing and not to do the other, and assume that the child already sees itself as an acting subject. But it is only through the process of praise and censure that those doing the rearing produce in children the consciousness that they are initiators of action, that they are the ones who have *received* and *merited* the praise and censure for particular actions. This unintentional influence on a child during the process of its education is the rule rather than the exception. If an adult wants to prevent a child from doing something again, they can yell, wag their finger threateningly, maybe even smack.

The child learns not only that this is something it should not do again, but it also learns that you yell, threaten and smack others when they do something you do not want them to do. If an adult makes a long, moralizing speech to convince an elder child of the correctness of a particular attitude, the child not only learns that certain attitudes are considered good, but it also learns to make long, moralizing speeches, etc. This means that the tools used for child-rearing have other effects on children in addition to those intended by the person using these tools to educate.

The unintended consequences of bringing up children with such tools are particularly evident during *language acquisition*. Parents teach their children that a dog is called 'dog', a table 'table' and an apple 'apple'. At some point the child will then say, 'Johnny wants the apple on the table.' In all probability most parents do not deliberately make the child learn the word 'I'. But because it is permanently exposed to parental language, it also learns, almost incidentally, the use of so-called indexical terms such as 'here', 'now' and 'I'. The ability to use these linguistic expressions gives rise to the ability to contemplate. This means that the ability to think about a being who has done, perceived and felt this or that is partly engendered by the ability to feel pride and remorse about an action because we have been praised or censured for it, and to use the word 'I' correctly.

Rather loftily, therefore, we can say that the consciousness of being an acting subject and self-awareness are products or constructs of an upbringing using language. A being which has no such linguistic education would find it hard to develop this sort of consciousness or would have to do it in another way. (It is not inconceivable that there are other means of developing these skills, but in us humans they probably come about in this way.) We cannot conclude from this reasoning that the 'I' is not real, but 'merely' a human construct. Talk of 'mere human constructs' only makes sense when we differentiate between elements of reality whose existence is dependent on other things and *absolute* things that exist in themselves. If, however, we admit that everything that really exists is dependent or contingent, the results of human actions, whether they have been produced intentionally or unintentionally, are no less real than the things which materialize independently from human action, but in relation to other things.

The development of a person's eyes and ears is dependent on the genes and the supply of food available to an embryo. If the genes 'responsible' for the development of eyes and ears are damaged or if the umbilical cord is blocked in the womb, no eyes and ears will develop. If a child has an upbringing where there is no praise and censure (like Kaspar Hauser) it does not develop a consciousness of being an acting subject. If it does not learn how to use self-reflexive words such as 'here', 'now' and 'I' it will have no self-awareness. Consciousness of being an agent and self-awareness are just as real as eyes and ears, even though they develop as a result of human acts of upbringing and language, rather than in relation to things such as genes and nutrition, and despite the fact that they are harder to see because we cannot yet identify the neurological differences between a being with an awareness of agency and self-awareness, and one without (but at some point we will probably be able to do this).

It is a fundamental error to see human constructs as unreal. Houses, bombs and factories are human constructs. Does this mean they are not real? If houses collapse, bombs are dropped and factories explode, people may die. Is there a more impressive proof of something real than the death of people? Hardly. What we have intentionally brought about as acting people is no less real than what has emerged independently of us. Steven Weinberg has rightly emphasized this point time and again in his writings.

Human relations bring about consciousness of action and self-reflectivity, and human relations are where ambition and vanity develop. As mentioned above, ambition and vanity are key elements of the dynamic of our society, which can even be seen in their external material development. Airports, skyscrapers, congress centres, sports stadiums and television broadcasters are all the result of the human emotions of ambition and vanity. Without these emotions those material constructs would not exist, while by the same token those material constructs have an effect on human emotions. Anybody who flies in a jet from one metropolis to another, looks out over a city from a glass office on the top floor of a skyscraper, makes a speech to hundreds of people in a congress centre, wins a victory in a large sports arena in front of thousands of spectators, or appears in a television broadcast and is seen by millions of people, can satisfy their ambition and vanity but also feel pleasure. This only feeds and increases their ambition and vanity, because the perception of their person and actions incurs a large material expenditure.

The need to see ourselves as autonomous subjects and to 'project' ourselves as an acting subject in the world – influencing many different outcomes and thereby affirming our presence in this world – stems from unease over our impotence, which implies our own contingency and finitude. The many conditions which make possible what I am now can vanish again – and me with them. It seems, therefore, that *denying* our own contingency may offer a protection against this danger. But what am I as an autonomous, absolute subject? The intangibility of the absolute 'removes' me from the world of the contingent – which is the only world we know. Hence the need to objectivize ourselves in the world of finite contingencies. The more the subject imagines itself as transcendent, the more it needs to affirm its reality in the world of experience via ever 'greater' influence. In fact, the continuity between the contingencies of the world and those which constitute the process of our existence is considerable. At first air is what surrounds us; after we breathe it becomes part of our blood. At first the word surrounds the subject; then it becomes part of their thinking. There is no strict boundary between the organism and its environment or between the contingent subject and its world. Just as changeable as the contingent relations of the world is the life process of organisms and subjects. It is precisely in this mutability that we find the key to happiness, which has nothing to do with the genesis or survival of organisms and subjects.

The present

Although human life is nothing more than a succession of present moments, most people almost never have a conscious experience of focusing on the present, or perhaps only in childhood. For the child-rearing process outlined above, which uses the mechanisms of reward and punishment, aims to teach the human mind to make *connections*: this action follows that; that action follows this. As actions, events acquire a value if they are associated through praise and censure with consequences, and if language which guides consciousness produces the connection between an action and its consequences, which might not occur until much later.

People's subjective experience, therefore, always extends over periods of time which vary in length. Children inhabit a narrow temporal horizon, whereas old people inhabit a broad one. When attention is spread over a broad horizon it appears to be *weakened*. It seems that, in a typical state of alertness relative to their disposition, people have a certain level of intensity of attentiveness, an intensity which can be spread over a narrow or broad horizon. If their attention is spread over a broad horizon it is 'thinner', just as a mass of cake dough is thinner if you roll it out over a large area than a smaller one.

The clarity and incisiveness with which something is perceived depends on the intensity of the focus you direct at it. The emotions, too, which are bound up with the perception of something, depend on the temporal horizon in which it is perceived. Something can be perceived as a *trace* of something that has passed, or as a *notification* of something in the future. For example, a face can appear in my memory. I can recall it as the face of a person who once caused me trouble and on whom I would like to take revenge for the trouble they caused me. In this case the facial features will not appear so clearly in my consciousness, just as I would be hardly conscious of the typeface of the letters used to write an interesting text. I will principally be thinking of the cause of the trouble and my future revenge; the face crops up only as a sign mediating between this past and this future.

The temporal experience of people who experience processes of reward and punishment, who in psychological terminology are 'conditioned' is largely characterized by the fact that one experience *refers* to another. Just as linguistic expressions represent networks of references, in which one letter has reference to another, one word to another, one sentence to another, one paragraph to another, for most of us our experiences refer to other experiences. To understand a sentence you not only need to make out the word that is sounding or being read right now, but also to retain what was just said, what was just read. Likewise, almost every experience evokes a memory or allows the anticipation of something in the future. We can also *infer* the cause of a current experience or the effects an experience will have in the future. Inferential and narrative relations are typical of our experiences and generally it is regarded as *positive* that we see things in context rather than in isolation. It is no coincidence that the same word – 'consequence' – is used to describe the fact that an action, depending on whether it is rewarded or punished, has nice, pleasure-related *consequences*, or unpleasant, pain-related ones for us as children, and that true or false *consequences* can be inferred from a premise. Criminal laws stipulate the *consequences* of particular actions: 'Murder will be punished by a custodial sentence of not less than fifteen years.' Logical laws determine end results: 'P and Q imply P.'

Establishing these sorts of relations has its consequences, however. What is experienced in the present becomes a *means of transition* from the past or into the future. In referential contexts the present shows what has happened, what will be, or both. Moreover, the contexts established by humans are based on particular *ideals*. This is seen most clearly with formal proof. It is either *complete* and *successful* or *incomplete* and *unsuccessful*. The individual elements of proof only have a value when they appear in the referential context of the conclusions of complete and successful proof.

How the relevance of a 'habitual' present is perceived very much depends on whether it occurs in a referential context and, if so, in which one. The colour green as an eye colour in a portrait or as a wall colour spread over several square metres is perceived completely differently (as Goethe once observed). A note which is heard for a fraction of a second within the referential context of a melody produces a different experience from that created by the same note resounding incessantly over the course of several minutes. If the word 'haddock' is registered in the sentence 'Yesterday I caught a haddock on the sandbank', this is an utterly different experience from the frequent repetition of the word, at the end of which the meaning no longer appears to be present, only the sound of the word (haddock, haddock, haddock, haddock, haddock . . . '). What happens with these spatial and temporal extensions of colours, notes and repeated signs is the loss of the *referential contexts* in which they originally stood or to which they are thought to belong when they occur in isolation. A single note may evoke the memory of a melody which begins with this. But if it is heard uninterruptedly for several minutes, it suppresses the melody, it stops being a sign *pars pro toto* for this melody. We generally feel that this lack of context 'distorts the meaning'.

We usually regard our own life as a context which we plan ourselves, or which a deity has planned for us, in which one thing follows on from another, which can succeed or fail, i.e., which in an ideal scenario is perceived as a whole and can be narrated. Even if we know that our own life consists of nothing but a succession of experiences of the present, we nonetheless integrate these into the context of our life by making reference in particular to memories and expectations, and asking ourselves, for example, whether what once happened will now happen again, or whether what is happening now is the 'right step' along the way to what we are hoping for.

Scholarly teachings from Indian and European antiquity to the present, however, have all along emphasized the importance to human life of experiencing the living present. Here, for example, is an observation from Ludwig Wittgenstein: 'If by eternity is understood not endless temporal duration but timelessness, then he lives eternally who lives in the present.' This phrase recalls the poem by Angelus Silesius: 'I myself am eternity / when I abandon time / And unite myself in God / and God in me.' If we observe the practices by which people are said to develop the ability to experience the living present, we see that they strive for something which is the *antithesis* to the positive evaluation of referential contexts.

If, during the course of Buddhist meditation, the instruction is given to focus on how breath enters and exits the body through the nose, caressing the upper lip and nostrils; if during this concentration on breathing, the memories, expectations and emotions which enter the mind of the person meditating are not powerfully suppressed, but not given any attention either – in contrast to the breath caressing the nostrils at that moment – it becomes clear that experiences are being *decontextualized*, they are being separated from the larger-scale life contexts gauged by particular ideals of totality. The focus on breathing is not to establish whether it is functioning *properly*. It is not used as a sign (as a doctor might use it) to check whether the person is *still alive* or, as its speed can reveal, in a *particular emotional state*. It is observed as something which is happening right now, but which need not refer to anything if the relevant contexts are not made or if they are disregarded. By focusing on breathing, the referential contexts which the conditioned mind creates for itself out of habit will increasingly be ignored, until all attention is directed to the physical sensations triggered by the breathing movements.

Because breathing has hardly any association with memories and expectations it is very boring to begin with. It seems as if people's attention normally requires more, requires something interesting, i.e., something which has meaning because it refers to something else, especially if it signifies something which might realize the ideal of the totality of our life. The news that this or that person loves or hates me, that I can pursue this or that activity, that I have got a job, may be conveyed with the same sort of breathing which I, sitting still in meditation, focus on as it enters and exits my nose. But because in the former instance this breathing is the medium for conveying information, information which has a certain meaning in my life, I do not perceive it as breathing, but only as the meaning which it transports. If, on the other hand, a person succeeds, after frequent, extensive and also strenuous practice of concentration, in actually perceiving the process of breathing over a considerable period of time and keeping all meaning at a distance, an astonishing feeling of happiness can set in which comes as a shock to many people. Suddenly, the feelings that are associated with breathing are no longer perceived as banal and boring because they do not refer to anything; on the contrary, the experience of the presence of breathing feels extraordinarily incisive and real, whereas the meaning something has within the context of an ideal life plan, be it focused on wealth, power or pleasure, all of a sudden appears insipid, unreal and ephemeral.

It is the objective of many scholarly teachings to train this ability, to narrow people's focus to the real things happening right now, independent of the units of meaning created by life plans, and to prevent the evasion of this living present by flight into referential contexts. The practices of these scholarly teachings often include the conscious destruction of meaning and referential contexts through paradoxes, bringing the mind to a halt by giving the instruction, for example, to clap with the left hand. From time immemorial it may have been crucial to man's survival that we remember and anticipate; indeed, the ability to remember was understood by Aristotle to be the very genesis of mental activity. But, according to many philosophers, and endorsed by many happiness practices, the ability to observe, to focus one's whole attention on what is happening right now, without seeing it *as something* which stands for *something else* apart from itself – this ability to observe is the basis for an attitude towards life which leads to a happy existence. Most of the things which make people unhappy stem from their bad memories, their expectations, anxieties and fears, and from the ideas of completeness and perfection which either they have developed from the referential context of their life or which they have learned from their culture.

To put it in general terms, we could say that the happiness represented by peace of mind depends on the ability to exist without worries. Being carefree means that the contexts of memory and expectation are relegated to *secondary* importance in a person's life, and experiencing the present moment becomes *primary*. To achieve this, our focus on what is present right now must be stabilized so that we can still maintain it when we *need* to remember and anticipate because our normal life circumstances demand this.

This prioritization – focusing *first* on the living present, and *then* mentally following referential contexts into the past and future – is only possible when our survival is relatively secure. A life under threat, suffering from a lack of food and pursued by enemies, is unlikely to be in a position to set these priorities. We must bear in mind, however, that the threat is not fixed at the same level for everybody. An entrepreneur trying to acquire a number of factories and earn a fortune may, if they identify with this economic empire, if it constitutes their 'extended ego', feel 'a threat to their existence', even though they will never have to suffer hunger and nobody is after their life just because their economic empire is threatened with collapse. An academic who has spent twenty-five years of their life on a piece of work and now realizes that they set out from false premises, may, if they identify themselves with this piece of work – if it constitutes 'their life' – feel a threat to their existence the moment these false premises become apparent.

The entrepreneur and academic are in a different situation from the nomadic Neanderthal who spends the nights in caves with their clan, faces the threat of being gobbled up by a leopard, and does not know whether they will find sufficient food the next day. But the concern that the prehistoric nomad feels for their life may not differ in its quality and intensity from that felt by the entrepreneur and scholar. As people become self-aware and conscious of their agency, and as the ego grows, the emotions associated with the organism's elementary struggle for survival, and which keep the search for food and the hunt for sexual partners going, are transferred to all sorts of other things. In many traditional teachings, therefore, the *prerequisite* for a practice of focusing on the present is a melting down of self-awareness, of consciousness of agency and of ego expansion. One way of doing this is to leave one's family and relinquish all possessions, as happens in some religious orders.

Members of some orders are then reliant on being able to satisfy their most basic survival needs by begging for food. In addition to having no personal possessions, some also refuse to become used to living in one place, where their survival interests and thus their concerns could unfold, and so they need to be perpetually on the move.

A key aspect of the strict training in focusing on the present – or de-education – is the de-conditioning of the connections in the mind which have given rise to self-awareness and consciousness of agency. Of course, it is not possible to make someone lose the mastery of the word 'I' once it has been acquired. But it is certainly possible to follow practices in which the tendency to see oneself as an acting subject, as the being which has developed from the actions of praise and censure is sharply curbed.

If an unpleasant, painful situation arises, survival interests and childhood conditioning mean that this is associated with two thoughts: 'Something dangerous might happen to me' and 'If I feel such pain I must have done something wrong; it must be a punishment for something.' The conclusions drawn from these ideas are that pain must be avoided, to escape the threat to one's survival and to remove oneself from the faulty situation. If, however, meditation practices demand that the pain which you feel in the knees – if, for example, you remain in a particular position for a long time – should not be avoided, that you should not change what you are doing but experience the pain; if the instruction is merely to perceive the feeling of threat which might arise, but not to react to it, this results after a while in a 'reconditioning'. It becomes clear that pain and trepidation are not necessarily associated with one's demise or punishment for a transgression, mistakes and suchlike, that they do not have to be related back to a 'self' or 'I' as a subject to be praised or chastised, but that they can be observed as *events in the world*.

In many scholarly teachings this 'melting down' of self-awareness is an element of developing the ability to experience the present. For example, the aforementioned Angelus Silesius writes: 'O Man, / While you still exist, / know, / have and love; believe me / you are not yet / delivered of your burden . . . Death is a blessed thing; the more powerful it is, the more magnificent will be the life that springs from it. By dying a thousand times the wise man / through truth appeals for a thousand lives.'

If an I-consciousness is seen as a fundamental, autonomous reality, there will also be concern about its survival. Once it is acknowledged as something that has appeared and that can disappear again – although this, in itself, is a source of worry because the I feels under threat – the probability of perceiving the present is increased. When Angelus Silesius talks of 'death', he probably means a de-education from a strong notion of the I. For this notion of the I produces 'burdens': the I has a character – it knows something, it loves something, it possesses something, and all of this can be lost. Fear of loss is ever present to a greater or lesser degree, as a dormant concern or as all-out panic. Until this tendency is overcome, experiencing, perceiving the present can only be of short duration. It is no longer possible when there is intense pain or the threat of death.

The weakening of the I-consciousness does not have to occur by means of ascetic practices in spiritual contexts. Mastering a musical instrument or a sporting manoeuvre can also raise the probability of perceiving the present, at least to a certain degree. It is known that playing music can bring about a complete focusing of attention on the sound, and that the execution of a complicated body movement can lead to an absolute concentration on this movement. People often report being totally lost in what they were doing and no longer experiencing the passing of time. Such activities are only possible when there is no threat to our survival. Despite the security, however, these non-spiritual practices can also be 'reversed'. If a musician loses themselves completely in their playing, a painter in their painting, a mathematician in their calculations, etc., but afterwards the individuals concerned are *praised* for what they have done, they can turn the total focus, the perception of the present in these activities into a *means of extending the ego*. Then it is hard to say whether the pianist is playing the piano on stage for the sake of playing piano or because they are activating in their lives a phase of piano-playing in order to have success, to be celebrated. An outside observer will find it impossible to tell whether a rower is focusing all their attention on the movement of their boat and is utterly lost in this focus, or whether they are trying to achieve this boat-focus to go as quickly as possible and win the race.

In principle, almost every activity can be undertaken for its own sake or for the sake of something else, i.e., either it gives rise to a living present or it is a means to an end, which, in the terminology of Aristotelian philosophy, is *practice* or *technique*. A window-cleaner cleans windows essentially to earn money; the motion of window-cleaning is a means to an end. But they can also 'lose themselves' in the motion of window-cleaning to such an extent that they do it for its own sake. 'From the outside' we cannot see the 'inner attitude' with which an activity is being undertaken. And yet a variety of activities have been established outside of spiritual institutions with different intentions. The difference between work, art and sport is probably also the difference between activities which are undertaken for survival and those which are carried out for their own sake, even though artistic and sporting activities in wealthy capitalist societies have now become highly oriented towards money and competition. This need not, however, prevent anybody from doing these or any other activity for its own sake to improve their ability to perceive the present.

Of course, these 'leisure activities' do not establish any permanent priority of present-focused experience over cares and worries. The perpetuation of a reflexive activity is only possible where, with every sense and movement, the initial perception is *the fact that* at that particular moment the brain is perceiving and the body moving. Only afterwards should we concern ourselves with *what* has been perceived and to what end we have acted. Prioritizing a focus on the present means that someone who sees a face first perceives that they are seeing a face, and only afterwards perceives what face they are looking at; that someone walking to the garden gate first perceives that they are walking and only afterwards that they are going to the garden gate. 'Normal' life is constituted in such a way that we perceive meanings and contexts of meaning, that we target objectives for our actions and try to realize them. Only in 'time-outs' do perceptions and movements take place for their own sakes – the violin is perceived as a sound rather than a meaning, swimming as a movement rather than a progression to a particular place – allowing a 'care-free' experiencing of the present. Anybody who wishes to achieve this prioritization of present-focused experience in all aspects of their life must practice regularly focusing on the present, ignoring referential contexts or contexts of anxiety, in order to develop a permanent skill of reflection or observation, or – if we believe the Buddhists that it has always existed (as the 'nature of the Buddha') – 'uncover' and 'awaken' it. To be able to practise this we need a great deal of freedom and to be unburdened from the worries of biological survival.

Freedom

Those beings who are either unaware of death or do not fear it are probably the most free of worries. This is why Spinoza argues that sensible people think of anything else but death. A person living in a modern wealthy society has many symbolically created identities which can be emotionally 'defended' almost as doggedly as their biological identity. Reports of people who commit suicide because they cannot pay back gambling debts, or because they have destroyed one of their social identities by another means are common. As a person's social identities become more complex the risk increases that they cannot maintain themselves as the being they have become. Their anxiety likewise increases. A first step on the path to freedom from worry, therefore, is the dismantling of social identities. Spiritual communities, such as monasteries, demand that applicants leave their families and jobs before entering the community. This liberates the person concerned from the most fundamental social identities, on which other identities are built. Leaving the world of complex referential contexts, they enter a simple social world, thereby giving themselves the opportunity for more frequent and more intense, present-focused perception.

Some spiritual communities also try to eliminate concern over biological survival. Not only by attempting to wean people off their sexual urges, but also by begging for food, rather than it being provided as a result of the individual's own labour. The time and latitude this frees up is massive, allowing this time to be used for present-focused perception in meditation exercises which take up the majority of the day. Such monastic freedom has been criticized for two reasons: first, it impoverishes human life because people no longer form any of the close and loving relationships which are usual in families; second, monastic freedom and the potential happiness generated by focusing on the present is parasitic on the lives of people who provide the food for the beggars.

If, as Aristotle and his successors did, you take as the measure of human existence the fullness of a life of joy and suffering determined by the ideal of biological survival of the self and species, then a life that strives for present-focused experience and seeks out the happiness of peace of mind in freedom from all worries is an impoverished one. If, however, we accept that the biological survival of the self and one's species is not compatible with happiness, because it necessarily leads to intense worry, then we can reject the idea of using this yardstick to measure our life. The question that then needs to be answered is: do we want to renounce happiness in order to satisfy our biological identity? Because we cannot control the emergence of our own biological identity – after all, we play no part in the arrival of our organic existence; we appear in this world as a result of our parents' reproductive actions – for all of us our biological identity is *preset*. When we *first* arrive in the world we harbour all the aspirations and desires of self and species survival. The question is whether, starting with this biological identity, we want to construct an even more complex system of identities and needs, or after experiencing the worries that are bound up with this identity we distance ourselves from the desire to fulfil our biological potential as thoroughly as possible.

To be in a position to achieve such a distance, we must be able to harness the real opportunity of *another* existence than that determined by the ideal of self and species survival. The communities of those who have committed themselves to the happiness of present-focused experience not only offer a model for life, according to which it is possible to distance oneself from one's biological identity; over the course of the centuries they have also developed many practices which could be helpful, both for their own members and also for people who still need to worry about survival. If everybody distanced themselves from their biological identity, humanity would disappear from the globe. If everybody sought only to realize their biological identity, there would be no idea of the possibility of human happiness and no tried-and-tested practices to attain this. We must not see the coexistence of an anxious, biologically determined life and the life in pursuit of happiness as a parasitic relationship in which those striving for peace of mind exist at the expense of those who work and worry. Rather we can describe this relationship as a *symbiotic* one, in which one partner provides the other with a livelihood permitting the freedom to investigate and pass on practices of self-liberation towards happiness. These represent a possibility for all people.

Lalitha Dakini
Niranjana

CHAPTER FOUR

Happiness is impossible, but the truth is beautiful

The problem

In the Western world at least it appears to be beyond dispute that we want to be happy; indeed, we have to be happy if our aim is to lead a good life. This has been the view since Aristotle's *Nichomachean Ethics*, if not earlier. The Indians and Chinese, and pessimistic philosophers in Europe such as Schopenhauer and his successors, have seen things differently, although for most of 'us' happiness is important and allegedly *possible*, too. For why should people strive for something which they do not believe is possible? It seems equally clear, however, that neither life from a purely biological perspective, nor life in human culture leads to happiness. Identifying and pursuing happiness is only possible, therefore, if we protect ourselves against those 'pitfalls' of biological life and civilization which prevent happiness.

In this study I will attempt to show that such a project is *impossible*. There is no process of reflection or behaviour which can free us from the basic biological and cultural determinants of our own lives, not even in philosophy. If this observation is right and if it is also true that our biological and cultural existence makes happiness impossible, then the idea of happiness is not an attainable goal, but an *unrealistic fantasy*. The attempt to realize unrealistic fantasies is a mistake, primarily because this strategy can only ever result in a sense of *failure*.

Imagine for a moment that I tell a child it ought to be able to jump nine metres in one go. It does not succeed. I am surprised and tell it again that it *must* be able to do it. In this way I will drive the child to *despair*. The same is true of the adult who thinks they have to be happy. They either despair or they pretend to be happy, even though they are not, even though their life does not correspond to the fantasies they have concocted about it, because others have told them that they should concoct such fantasies. The only improvement in life we humans can effect is to be freed from the pressure to believe we have to achieve something impossible. I will argue that *this* is the improvement we should strive for instead of trying to attain 'consummate happiness'.

In people's futile search for happiness, abstract notions of 'nature' and 'culture' have often played a key role. Sometimes the natural conditions in which people exist have been identified as preventing happiness, and salvation has been sought in a refinement of civilization, especially in the sciences and the acceleration of its progress; sometimes civilization has been seen as corrupting, the ruin of mankind, and it has been argued that we need to return to nature to achieve happiness. But nature and culture do not exist as such. Can we recall a natural state? Perhaps it exists only as a diorama in natural history museums where artificial Neanderthals that we regard as humans sit around a fire. And where is the civilization that allows us to escape nature? Major floods, storms, earthquakes and meteorites can destroy the most modern buildings and technical facilities, indeed the entire human species and all it has created. Which person has achieved immortality? Is death not a natural event?

These questions should show that it is impossible to draw a line between culture and nature. Out of desperation we consider the circumstances in which we have to live our lives and imagine a natural world in which once upon a time everything was better, or a civilization in which one day everything will be better. 'Nature' and 'culture' are ciphers for illusions in downfall and salvation narratives. The belief in happiness via a 'return to nature' feeds off the downfall narrative that we once existed in a natural state of paradise in which there was no suffering and no death, but from which we fell because of a sin. But the paradise of the Bible is not the natural world we know. Belief in technological progress in culture as the solution to all the problems of our natural existence is driven by the fantasy of a salvation narrative: there may be much suffering and catastrophe throughout the life of an individual, a tribe or the whole species. But in the end everything turns out fine. We are saved. We have learned from our mistakes and will attain happiness through technology. What evidence do we have that the history of mankind will follow such a narrative of salvation? Did it ultimately turn out fine for the dinosaurs? Why should any development in the world follow the direction of our interests? There is no evidence for a god who is there for us, looks after us, forgives our mistakes and ultimately saves us. Nor is there any evidence that we can save ourselves, that our ability to solve problems will triumph in the end, and that we will be able to avoid all the problems and catastrophes we have created for ourselves, or those which the world has prepared for us independently of our actions. These notions of paradise and salvation are mere fantasies which are supposed to substantiate the idea that happiness is possible. If we reject them, happiness becomes an unlikely prospect, too.

For this reason I will start by demonstrating why civilization cannot possibly make people happy, and then examine the constants of *biological* life and its incompatibility with the idea of happiness. I will conclude by discussing how life improves when we accept that happiness is impossible.

Civilization as a collective delusion

People create many types of patterns. One of these is the pattern of their individual life, another the one they produce together with others in large communities and which we call 'culture' or 'civilization'. Both types of pattern, the individual and the collective, are related, but seldom harmoniously. Often when creating their life pattern, the individual person feels obstructed by the ambitions of the community, or the community looks at the need of individuals to produce a particular pattern as a disruption. Recently, Imre Kertész expressed his serious doubts about the sense in collective pattern creation:

> I don't know when I first had the idea that some terrible delusion, a devilish irony must be at work in the world order, whereas you experience it as a normal, ordered life, and this terrible delusion is culture itself, the edifice of ideas, language and concepts which hide from you the fact that you have long been a well-oiled functioning part of the machinery created for your own destruction. The secret of survival is collaboration, but to admit this comes back at you as such a disgrace that instead of undertaking it, you prefer to leave it.

Like almost everything which Kertész writes, this quotation is formulated against the background of the Nazi concentration camps. But Kertész sees a fundamental connection between the camps and European civilization; in his self-questioning he continues:

> For this very context reveals the catastrophic significance of Auschwitz for people who grew up in the ethical culture of Europe. One of the laws laid down in the Ten Commandments in this culture is: thou shalt not kill. So, if mass murder becomes everyday practice, everyday work we might even say, then we must decide whether a culture whose illusory value system all of us here in Europe, murderers as well as victims, are taught from primary school onwards still has any validity.
>
> You are creating [Kertész remarks to himself] a nightmarish vision. With knapsacks on their backs, millions of children are trotting to school, only to meet again later as murderers and victims outside crematoriums, at pits dug as mass graves . . .
>
> It appears that when we start talking about culture and the European value system we soon arrive at the question of murder.

However it may sound on a first reading, Kertész is far from holding European culture *responsible* in some way for the mass murders of the twentieth century. How should an abstract notion like culture have responsibility? Kertész is merely noting the huge discrepancy between the ideals conveyed by European culture and the reality of this culture. The reason for this discrepancy could be an illusion about the mechanisms in the pattern-forming of individual lives or the fact that the forces of socialization have not yet been identified. Here is a final quotation from Kertész:

> It seems that neither people nor societies are born for *happiness*, but for *conflict*. The goal being pursued is always happiness, but it is only ever a seductive projection. We still do not know how individual life is compatible with the goals of society, about which we know precious little. We still do not know what drives us and why - beyond vegetative automatism - we actually live. Essentially the question of whether *we* exist or whether we are just figures of clusters of cells at work inside us that have become bodies - a phenomenon which behaves, is forced to behave, as if it were autonomous reality. To me, who is not important, something nevertheless is important which is not important . . .

In our culture happiness is important for almost everyone. Happiness and the truth are the two goals which people pursue both as individuals and in communities. Our hopes are directed to both these goals, as if the world must 'basically' be configured for human activity, thereby making happiness possible, just as it must 'tie in with' human cognitive faculties and these tie in with the world and permit the truth. But as individuals and communities we are forever deluding ourselves and finding ourselves in contexts in which it is impossible to pursue what we imagine to be happiness. Why is this the case? Is there no perspective from which the quest for happiness (and truth) is irrelevant? Did statesmen such as Lenin and so-called bearers of culture such as Nietzsche not believe that individual happiness could be sacrificed for the political or cultural advancement of humanity as a whole? From where did they get the certainty of their conviction that they were in possession of the truth, and what sort of future happiness were they striving for which gave them the right to sacrifice many lives for it in the present? *Which* truth exactly did they believe they possessed when convinced that this or that configuration of human circumstances in the future must lead to happiness? Is it not possible that happiness and truth – the notion of the 'fit' between human desires and knowledge on one hand, and the world on the other – is an illusory idea of mutual harmony, for which there is no proof? Is the premise of this hypothesis, that the world is *there* and human actions and knowledge *here*, not suspect in itself?

Not only Imre Kertész but Sigmund Freud, too, questioned the connection between individual human happiness and supposedly larger-scale perspectives of culture or nature, whoever adopts these. Both men gave similar answers, as did the seventeenth-century British philosopher Thomas Hobbes, who argued that happiness is a chimera, an illusion which cannot be attained in *any* context, neither an *individual* one nor a larger *natural* or *cultural* context. Hobbes had already reached the conclusion that all life processes are bound up with motion and that this motion expends resources. So long as we live we are threatened by the exhaustion of these resources. To access them we need to move; to move we need the resources. For Hobbes there is no way out of this vicious circle:

> For there is no such thing as perpetual Tranquillity of mind, while we live here; because Life itself is but Motion, and can never be without Desire, nor without Feare, no more than without Sense. What kind of Felicity God hath ordained to them that devoutly honour him, a man shall no sooner know, than enjoy; being joys, that now are as incomprehensible, as the word of School-men, Beatifical Vision, is unintelligible.

Hobbes's observation about the felicity which God has ordained for us is, of course, ironic. He can hardly have believed in an afterlife. His beatific vision is a life without movement, a life which expends no resources and thus has no need for resources or any concern about losing them. But a life without motion is a self-contradiction, according to Hobbes. Nor will culture – or in a Hobbesian context, the state – make us motionless movers, beings which can live without it costing them anything.

If things are so simple – and Hobbes's view of life has undoubtedly remained valid to the present day (indeed, the severity with which life is dependent on resources must be even more evident to us today than back then) – where does the idea of happiness and its attainability come from? Perhaps from the short period of childhood security; a vague, non-verbalizable memory. Maybe it is also a deception mechanism 'instilled' in children by adults to make them continue with life and take on its burdens. In Werner Herzog's film version of the story of Kaspar Hauser, who enters human civilization as an adolescent, having been locked for years in a dungeon without any human contact, Kaspar perceives his 'appearance in this world' as a 'heavy fall'. Before his violent death he has a vision which he recounts to those gathered around his deathbed: 'I saw the sea. I saw a mountain and many people climbing the mountain like a procession. It was very foggy. I couldn't see it clearly. And at the top was death.'

It seems that Kaspar Hauser did not espouse the idea of happiness which perhaps as children we are inoculated with as an implicit promise and life-long burden. For him the transition from dungeon to 'the world' is no improvement. The civilizing process he has to pass through by learning how to speak, eat properly and play the piano seems to him to be a strenuous collective mountain climb. As the film shows, the amorphous water, the natural point of origin of life, the semi-conscious bliss of floating in the amniotic sac is abandoned by people after birth on their path into civilization and replaced by a steep, rocky mountain. Like Kaspar himself, people suddenly have to learn much about training and thus strenuous endeavour. But in the end they die or – as in Kaspar Hauser's case and, if we recall Kertész's opening observation, millions of others, too – are killed. People exist for each other like wolves, Kaspar says on one occasion, horrifying his tutor. In Kaspar's vision the civilizing process takes place in the fog, without orientation; what is intended by it, where it is supposed to lead apart from death, remains unclear. In the final vision before his death – a caravan in the desert led by a blind old Berber, which stops by a mountain because the group thinks it has lost its way and is given no orientation by the compass – Kaspar again questions the collective motion of civilization as a blind drifting, which neither serves the individual nor leads collectively to a goal. He cannot understand the promise of happiness given by those who have brought him up following his time in the dungeon, even though he occasionally experiences moments of exhilaration like a child in nature; for example, when feeding an animal. He tries to imitate people's cultural behaviour, but he does not understand why, because he cannot understand the promise of happiness. In his final vision it seems as if he regards the whole of civilization as nothing but a delusion.

In spite of the attempts to civilize him, perhaps Kaspar remains an *honest* child. For children stick to those things that seem self-evident and refuse to be persuaded, not even by adults, of any evaluation of their circumstances which differs from what their senses are telling them. Children will not let themselves be persuaded that spinach is anything other than disgusting; they howl if they are forced to eat it. Cold water is not refreshing; they howl if they are made to sit in it. A small child lacks a perspective on education and culture overall. In Werner Herzog's film Kaspar seems to be adamant that his own opinions are right, just like a child who has not yet felt the need to flatter or impress anybody. On the other hand, prior to his death Kaspar has developed a perspective on the general programme of civilization. And Kaspar's verdict is a negative one: an aimless, meaningless, costly, collective motion, at the end of which is only death.

Disillusionment

Freud's treatment of 'uneasiness in civilization' has been called 'perhaps the last treatise on happiness'. It is undeniable that the question of defining happiness and its attainability is a fundamentally *philosophical* one, and in a sense it is clear that the Calenberg Academy is trying to make a connection with Freud, which is why it makes sense to refer back to him. Happiness has been a philosophical topic since Aristotle's writings on the *eudaimonia*. But it was not until the twentieth century – maybe not explicitly until Nietzsche and Freud – that a close connection seems to have been made between culture, nature and happiness. Similar to Kertész, however, Freud addresses this topic against a background which, however you define 'happiness', can only give rise to *resignation* as to its attainability. Freud is less interested in the question of *what sort of* civilization can help people find happiness than in the problem of why individual happiness and civilization do not appear to be *compatible*. Indeed, given the goals that cultures have, is there any point in speaking of individual happiness? Freud says no. Although *Civilization and its Discontents* was published in Germany in 1930, thus before the so-called Nazi 'takeover of power', it was written with the consciousness of the experiences of the First World War. For in this book Freud defines civilization as *an agency of protection against aggression* by individuals. He writes:

> Civilization . . . overcomes the individual's dangerous aggressive urges by weakening and disarming them and, by placing an agency inside the individual which watches over them like a garrison in a conquered city.

Freud expresses the same idea in his 1932 letter to Albert Einstein, 'Why war?', regarding civilization as a process of sensitization which makes war with its attendant horrors ever more unbearable. (This is analogous to Nietzsche's notion of an increasing decadence through the civilizing process, even though Freud's implicit assessment of the process is different from Nietzsche's.) People become too *sensitive* to be able to bear the bloodshed of war. It is not some sort of *insight* into the senselessness of war, which might fuel hopes that it could be eliminated as an institution. According to Freud the aggressive or death drive is too deeply rooted in the human constitution for this to happen. The civilizing process merely leads to a 'constitutional intolerance' against events on the battlefields, which turns civilized people into secondary pacifists emotionally (rather than intellectually), even if their basic drives do not make them naturally pacifistic.

According to Freud, the opportunity to 'play out' one's aggressive urges on a permanent basis, which war makes temporarily possible, would do as little to foster human happiness as culturally uninhibited sexual behaviour (itself always associated with aggression), removing the obstacles which separate the individual who feels sexual desire from the object of their desire. Ultimately, playing out one's aggressive urges would only lead to an increased threat, i.e., an insecurity of people in relation to each other, driving some to ever crueller *savagery* and others into ever greater *anxiety*. These are processes which can actually be observed in wartime. For this reason civilization is necessary. But according to Freud, the civilized person has 'exchanged a portion of potential happiness' offered by the urge for destruction and sexuality for a 'portion of security'. The satisfaction of our drives is never more than a *portion* of potential happiness, however, rather than *permanent happiness*, which exists only in the imagination as per Nietzsche's dictum that all desire 'aspires to eternity'. Even a pacified culture offers only a *portion* of security, no true or eternal security, because the threat of war can arise at any moment.

Natural circumstances do not allow people to be happy because, as Freud says, the *natural–biological disposition* of humans itself entails unhappiness. According to Freud, the phrase 'Life as it is set out for us is too difficult, it gives us too much pain, disappointment, unsolvable tasks,' does not apply in the first instance to man's cultural existence, but to his *natural* one. Our inner emotional complexity, which manifests itself, for example, in the necessary (as Freud sees it) contradiction of the Thanatos and Eros drives – where aggressive tendencies that go as far as targeting self-obliteration are in permanent conflict with other productive endeavours that aim to unite – does not allow us, as natural beings, to enjoy happiness in the sense of peaceful, fulfilled activity. Freud seems to have a similar view of the natural situation of human beings to Thomas Hobbes, but one which is darker still, for like Hobbes he not only considers food resources, but sexuality, too, and the destructive tendencies that both contradict and support it. The internal complexity of the natural person increases from Hobbes to Freud. In addition to demand and fear, Freud's work explores the urges for destruction and fusion. The objects of desire we want to fuse with are only attainable if we remove many obstacles. But the more efficient we are in eliminating the obstacles, the more aggressive our disposition, the less capable we are of falling into a state of union and being peaceful. Even the emotional structure underpinning the conservation of our species is, according to Freud, self-contradictory and anything but a facilitator of happiness. Thus we have defined the 'coordinates' in which Freudian thinking about civilization takes place: culture which offers security, the contradictory drives of humans, and above both of these the fantasy of happiness. Based on these three axes Freud observes human life in a way which is still illuminating for us today.

Freud as a philosopher

Some people might find it surprising that Freud, in relation to his theoretical writing on civilization, is being treated as a philosopher who has something valid to say about whether people can be happy and, if so, how. But there are several reasons for doing so. The first is *epistemological*; the second, which I will discuss later, relates to his analysis of *ethics*.

The epistemological reason relates to Freud's approach to *truth*. Here I do not mean the scientific truth of the psychoanalytical theory of drives. This is known to be controversial within clinical psychology and psychiatry, and even psychoanalysis has progressed beyond his theory now. The question as to whether psychoanalysis is true in the sense of scientific acceptance is not of interest here, as it cannot be determined by philosophy alone. Of far more interest is the truth of the *evaluation of the cultural and natural existence of mankind*, which Freud undertakes as a backdrop to his therapeutic work. Looking at psychoanalysis merely as a form of therapy can mean viewing it as a *technique* for eliminating suffering, which has nothing to do with understanding the true circumstances. One self-deception may be replaced by another, so long as the new deception is useful for the suffering person seeking help from the therapist. However, such an *instrumental* interpretation (to use a scientific term) of psychoanalysis does not fit Freud's understanding of his work.

This is clear from the famous '*Junktim*' or conjunction idea in individual psychology, according to which a successful cure is always accompanied by an advance in knowledge; indeed, the healing of a neurosis by the psychoanalyst *requires* an advance in knowledge. This idea is not compatible with an instrumental understanding of psychoanalysis, because if a technique that does not work needs to be modified and adjusted, it does not necessarily imply an expansion of knowledge. Such an expansion of knowledge is necessary in psychoanalysis, however, because each case manifests itself slightly differently and never corresponds entirely to the theoretical notions. If you cannot knock a nail into a concrete wall with a small hammer you reach for a heavier hammer. Apart from the realization that the task cannot be completed with the small hammer, there is not necessarily much insight gleaned into the individual conditions of the wall and nail.

The claim to knowledge connected with Freud's project is seen more clearly in his theoretical writings on culture than in individual psychopathology. The very title of his second great work on this topic, *The Future of an Illusion*, makes this evident. Freud looks at *disillusionment* and *strength* at the level of civilization and the individual. For Freud sees illusions as a sign of weakness, which reality as it is constituted cannot tolerate. There is no sense in disillusioning someone who is not capable of stomaching the truth. They would either perish or replace the old illusion with a new and different one in order to keep themselves alive. The question of having the strength to cope with the truth is one of *power*. The wish to acquire this power at all only makes sense when it is independent of the quest for happiness, where truth itself is seen as a *value*.

We know from both Nietzsche and Ibsen that the truth is not a requirement for relieving suffering; it is not even necessary for survival. On the contrary, it can be dangerous and cause suffering. Those interested only in survival and the good life need not care whether they exist in an illusion so long as it works for them. It only makes sense to destroy the illusion and carry on life's struggle without it when a good life with the illusion is considered *worse* than a difficult one with the truth. If, however, neither the natural life nor civilization can make happiness possible, then truth must represent a value *beyond* happiness. That is exactly what Freud seems to think. He appears, therefore, to share the philosophical conviction of John Stuart Mill that it is better to be an unhappy Socrates than a happy pig. But then he cannot view his psychoanalysis just as a *technique* which might also relieve suffering with illusions.

In the context we are looking at here, when Freud refers to illusion he means *religion*. He defines an illusion as a particular type of delusion: a delusion which is supposed to fulfil a wish, but in fact only succeeds in disguising the unfulfillability of the wish. According to Freud, the strength of religion as a determining factor of civilization lies in the strength of the wishes it promises to fulfil. These wishes scarcely seem to be satisfiable because they are so *urgent*. Freud believes that the religious illusion approaches the 'psychiatric notion of madness'. Freud calls a belief an illusion when 'in its motivation the wish-fulfilment pushes itself to the front', and the 'relationship to reality' recedes behind the wish-fulfilment, which is why the illusion can do without 'authentication'.

This talk of 'reality' and 'madness' of 'wish' and 'doing without authentication' is only understandable when Freud is also able to conceive of a *non*-illusory, i.e., *truthful* relationship to reality which demands authentication or confirmation.

In the face of an indifferent reality that makes them unhappy, people often feel helpless and powerless. In childhood this was compensated for by a strong father or another adult. The

Abrahamic religions promise to fulfil the desire that throughout the rest of their lives this be compensated for by a divine person who is greater, stronger, more powerful then themselves. Given how powerless people actually are, which manifests itself most horrifyingly in the fear of death, this desire is so intense that it is capable of invoking very sophisticated illusions which no lack of evidence can dispel.

The powerlessness of the individual in the face of reality is chiefly a result of the *indifference* of reality, the fact that it is not configured for the individual. This is true of nature as well as culture. In both cases the individual appears to be a simple contributor to, and bearer of, more complex processes, but never the goal. If the person's wishes are satisfied, it is not because these wishes are the end in themselves, but because the satisfaction of their needs is a means to another supposedly 'higher' natural or cultural end. A religion in which it is imagined that the individual's wishes are acknowledged and satisfied in a personal, one-to-one relationship, such as one may have with loving parents, compensates for the indifference of nature and culture towards the individual in a way which Freud calls 'regressive': by imagining the possibility of returning to childhood security under the watchful eye of parents. The physico-theological idea that sandy soils exist to grow conifers and potatoes, but that conifers and potatoes were designated by a god as human food and a building material – this assumed order of the world for human beings as the proof for the existence of a god is nothing more than a complicated fairy tale to maintain the self-delusion of security. For just as we can highlight those factors of nature which serve human interests, we can also point to the natural horrors, the venomous snakes and predators, earthquakes and volcanic eruptions, and, finally, the indifference of the cosmos in which stars are born and extinguished in rhythms of billions of years.

Whereas the family usually functions for the benefit of its individual members – even though one might question how its reproductive function benefits the individual – this is not at all the case in nature and civilization. Freud's thinking, like Spinoza's, is anti-teleological here: people believe that nature and civilization are *intentionally configured for them* or *geared towards them*. In truth, however, neither is. Therapy consists of acknowledging this truth and learning to live with it, i.e., shedding one's illusions. Freud does not, therefore, attempt an optimistic therapy, which, like Aristotle, contemplates the possibility of happiness in nature and culture, but a *therapy of resignation* which unmasks as an illusion the idea that happiness might be attainable. This brings in its wake many other illusions, including religious ones.

The most significant of these illusions is probably that of *immortality*. As far as Freud is concerned, death is unthinkable for the unconscious, the natural motor of the human psyche. This is why there is such a great tendency to accept myths, which, like Christianity, put forward the 'resurrection of the flesh'; or those like Platonism, which refer to an immortal soul as a substance that can detach itself from the dead body, even though not the slightest evidence exists that any of these are true. Even immortality myths which operate without substantive notions about the soul fulfil this desire for survival. The same function is performed by the Buddhist idea that although the whole, such as that of a body or a person, does not correspond to any reality, the small elements (*kalapas*) of which it consists do, and these never die. Here is the example sometimes given to illustrate this idea: the fact that the cloud does not disappear when it rains, but is transformed into drops of water, obscures the possibility of the *disappearance of a perspective*. The change from experience *with* the body to one *in* the body, in which this is immobilized through meditative restraint, partially blocks out a person's living perspective of the world, replacing it with a segmented one. Yet it is precisely this disappearance of 'large-scale' perspective – in which the world is experienced as a context through the interaction of the five senses with the body – that makes people fear death. The 'survival' of elementary particles, whether these be materially designed atoms or 'ontologically neutral' microelements only seems to replace the much-desired survival of this perspective.

Imagine a person who drops an expensive and well-loved Chinese vase and cries over the loss of this object, but then asserts that it is not broken, only transformed, or that its idea still exists in a divine spirit. We would be right to describe this person as neurotic or mad, as too weak to cope with the loss of the vase, which, after all, is a real loss. And yet millions of people behave in exactly the same way at the gravesides of their loved ones. Freud is surely right, therefore, when he describes religion as a psychopathological mindset resulting from the human inability to cope with the world as it actually is. From this assessment that religion is an illusory, but extremely relevant force of influence in civilization, Freud arrives at a *general suspicion* of the institutions in culture, which seems to correspond with the mistrust expressed by Kertész in the quotation cited above, although it is formulated less radically:

> Once we have recognized religious teachings as illusions, we are immediately faced with the further question of whether other cultural possessions which we venerate and allow to dominate our lives are similar in nature. Do the premises that govern our state institutions also need to be labelled as illusions? Are the relations between the sexes in our culture not clouded by one or more erotic illusions?

It is well known that Freud viewed the cultivation of the erotic with mistrust. Its objective is not the happiness of those individuals concerned, but the satisfaction of society by eliminating competitive conflict. Freud's mistrust of the illusory character of perhaps all elements of civilization stops at *science*, however. Science for him cannot be something that fulfils wishes in an illusory way, because its progress is too slow, impeded by too many obstacles, and it sets too much store by proof, which might invalidate a pleasant, wish-fulfilling truth. At the same time, however, Freud believes that the search for proof, which underpins science, harbours something that connects people more strongly than their natural drives and cultural networks: reason.

> There is no agency higher than reason. If the truth of religious teachings is dependent on an inner experience which bears witness to that truth, what are we to do with the mass of people that lack such an experience? We can demand that everyone use the gift of reason that they possess, but we cannot create an obligation applicable to everyone based on a motive that exists for very few. One person might enter a profound state of ecstasy and from it develop

> the unshakeable conviction of the real veracity of religious teachings, but what does that mean to another person?

Whereas people's erotic attachments lead to *competition* if two people desire a third person (or at best to *indifference* if one person cannot relate to another's desires, which, although they may promise the latter happiness, appear alien to the former) and whereas religious ecstasy is a private, inner experience, for Freud *reason* is something *universal* shared by all of us, potentially at least. On this point he is in agreement with Enlightenment philosophers such as Descartes and Kant. In any event Freud views the 'voice of the intellect' as a quiet one, which is only seldom able to compete with human drives and the tendency towards wish-fulfilment in determining action. And yet the truth seems to him more important than the pleasant feelings that the illusion of happiness sometimes appears to create. We should agree with Freud here.

Conscience and the impossibility of happiness

It has already been noted that Freud identifies civilization as a means of subduing aggressive human tendencies. As we have seen, in Freud's eyes civilization overcomes 'the individual's aggressive urges', weakening their physical and emotional powers by removing many of life's hardships. In this way the individual is ultimately 'disarmed' and civilization's norms establish an 'agency in their inner selves', which 'watches over them like a garrison in a conquered city'. The agency of supervision that civilization installs to control aggression is the *conscience* or, as Freud calls it, the 'superego'. Within this mental agency, the internalized moral concepts that people adopt from their parents in childhood keep a lifelong watch.

Before a child has been brought up by its parents this agency is absent. It marks the start of culture within the individual. On the one hand, parents are protectors and a source of attention. As we have seen, later on this role will continue to figure in religion, in illusory fantasies about a heavenly father, for example. On the other hand, parents are also the starting point for the civilizing of the individual: they produce an *inner structure*, create a mental complexity in which the childish desires of expansion and destruction are subdued and diverted.

And yet the creation of a conscience or 'superego' has its price: *the sense of guilt*. The civilized person turns the aggression which is no longer directed outwards back on themselves. The internal psychological complexity produced by the civilizing process is combative: the external conflict between aggressive individuals is transformed into an internal conflict between mental agencies.

Freud expresses the aim of his thinking in *Civilization and its Discontents* thus:

> It . . . does, however, correspond to my intention of representing the sense of guilt as the most important problem of cultural development and to show that the price of cultural progress is paid for by a *loss of happiness* that results from a heightened sense of guilt.

The child exhibits a natural aggression by taking pleasure in smashing crockery or hitting another child that covets its toy. The parents punishing the child show aggression by preventing the child from continuing to be aggressive – by restraining it, for example – and insisting that it is not allowed to behave like that. If the child learns its lesson it develops a bad conscience the moment it feels another aggressive impulse against things or other people. 'The aggression of the conscience,' Freud writes, 'preserves the aggression of authority.'

Civilizing does not, therefore, mean a *disappearance* of aggression, but a reshaping of it, whereby the aggression between people and that directed at created objects plays out within the individual, within their own mental life. To put it in a nutshell, *inter*-individual aggression becomes *inner*-individual aggression. If we use a rather trite categorization and say that aggression and destruction are bad, whereas mildness and construction are good, the civilizing process of a human being is in no way a development towards the good. It only seems as if the destructive nature of aggression is being eliminated from the world; in fact, it is just being 'swept under the carpet'. Instead of attacking other people and things, the civilized person directs their aggression towards their own drives. The impulse to act aggressively towards other people and things is aggressively combated inside, but this process of internalization in fact only increases the aggressive energy.

Once a conscience or superego has developed, according to Freud this internal complexity acquires its own dynamic. 'Every denial of a drive,' Freud writes, i.e., every inhibition or suppression of a culturally undesirable aggressive impulse, for example, 'now becomes a dynamic source of conscience; each new denial increases its severity and intolerance, and if we could relate it to what we already know about the genesis of conscience, we would be tempted to acknowledge the paradoxical phrase: conscience is the result of denying our drives, or the denial of drives (by an external impulse) creates the conscience which demands further denials of our drives.'

According to Freud, the successful use of the aggressive conscience to restrain aggression has the effect of *diverting* the aggressive tendencies – as his model of energy dynamics argues – away from the psychological agencies that are directed to the outside world, and towards the conscience. In successfully inhibiting drives, the conscience is strengthened by directing the suppressed energies towards itself. It is as if criminals were not only prevented from committing crimes by the police, but that they handed themselves into the police as a result of this prevention. This is an image used by Anthony Burgess in his novel *A Clockwork Orange*, in which the villains actually change sides: the violence they once waged as lawless youths they later use on their former gang leader as police officers.

If there is no need for the conscience to exert control and internalize aggression because civilization requires a 'natural' aggression to be directed externally, as in war situations or other group conflicts, the aggression suppressed culturally through upbringing suddenly becomes external and visible again. We have seen how Freud argues that the suppression of externally directed aggression makes the conscience more aggressive, and so inner aggression grows during the civilizing process. For Freud, therefore, we should not be surprised that a culturally peaceful phase can be followed by severe externally directed violence in wartime perpetrated by civilized individuals. For civilized individuals are not pacifists. On the contrary, their capacity for aggression has actually *increased* during the civilizing process due to a reinforced superego or conscience. All civilization has done is to refine their senses, thereby weakening the ability to tolerate external savagery associated with bloodshed. But their desire to commit it has not been erased, because they are familiar with the cruellest, non-bloody psychological savageries. If a religion stipulates that something should not be done and a conscience is trained according to this command, the aggression against those who do not observe the order may end up being more severe. Whereas in peaceful times only aggression against the self is practised and violence becomes almost cultivated, the moment the order is issued to one group to attack another because the latter has treated the prevailing rules and ideals with contempt, an intense violence towards external targets can be unleashed with fervour. Religious conflicts, such as that between Hindus and Muslims in India, can be seen as confirmation of this psychoanalytical notion. In Freud's time evidence for this thesis was provided by the euphoria with which the members of civilized nations entered the First World War and the savagery with which they slaughtered each other. Later, the ease with which highly cultured doctors took part in the crimes in Nazi concentration camps proved that the level of education someone had enjoyed was no predictor of the savageries they might be capable of.

What consequences does this theory of aggression have for our investigation into the possibility of human happiness? As long as individuals live in a state of *inner* conflict they are not happy, because either their drives or moral ideas are not being satisfied. Either they have a bad conscience or they are suffering from frustrated desires and needs. If the aggression is directed externally against *others* they may be freed from a bad conscience, but their life is threatened and they suffer from the fear of a war situation. Individual happiness would consist of *remaining true to one's moral ideals without denying one's drives* or *satisfying one's desires without a bad conscience*. But according to Freud this is impossible. For any return to a conscience-free state, quite apart from its unfeasibility, would only be a return to mutual threats and the resulting fear of one another. Hobbes had already shown that people will abandon a natural state as a permanent war of everybody against everybody the moment they realize the security advantages offered by creating a monopoly on violence. A peaceful integration of people in a civilization, on the other hand, is dependent on *binding the energies* which represent people's drives to allow cultural achievement. Such a constellation leads to an irresolvable conflict between the individual pursuit of happiness and collective cultural development. Although the individual always *hopes* that morality and life, their own needs and those of others, are compatible without conflict or competition, they repeatedly *discover* that this is impossible. Looked at realistically, even the peace of death does not promise any happiness.

Occasionally, Freud did admit that there was a drive in people to return to an inorganic state, a Nirvana principle or the death drive, as he called it. He saw this drive, too, as another cause of enthusiasm for war. The drive also conflicts with the life-affirming Eros drive, so that not only do conscience and instinct create an inner contradiction in human beings, but instinct is contradictory in itself. Freud was not totally sure of the plausibility of this hypothesis, however. On the other hand, the return of the individual to the peace of death, the dissolution of organic activity into inorganic does not promise happiness, but only an end to the unhappiness of life's contradictions. However, the power of the Eros drive, which keeps life going, always results in inner or external conflicts. This is what gives rise to the wish for a harmonious, almost drive-free existence and the illusion of the possibility of such an existence in life *after* death, which seems to fulfil this wish. Freud writes:

> Thus . . . the two urges, for individual happiness and for human company, have to compete within each individual, the two processes of individual and cultural development have to stand in hostile opposition to each other and argue the ground beneath them. But this conflict between individual and society is not the result of the likely irreconcilable contradiction between the primal drives of Eros and death; it signifies a dispute in the house of libido, comparable to the quarrel over the distribution of the libido between the ego and the objects, and it allows for a final settlement in the individual, as it does hopefully for the future of civilization, however much it may burden the life of the individual at present.

Ethics as a solution

In view of this dilemma of inner and outer conflicts, some philosophers place their faith in ethics. The *right* ethics must be found to bring people into agreement with themselves as well as with others. Then the individual quest for happiness and its necessary collectivization would be compatible. Such an idea assumes that ethics is a *problem-solving process* that seeks chiefly to solve the problem of how people can be happy. But as we know from mathematics there are problems which are solvable and those that are not. And there is no reason to believe that the problem of how people can be happy – with their natural drives and the need for civilization to restrain these – is really solvable.

The conflicts people enter into with themselves and others represent the first problem that needs to be solved in the quest for happiness. If this problem is solved then an ethics would already be very successful. In Freud's opinion, however, ethics is incapable of solving this problem. For him, ethics does not, in fact, solve any problems, but is part of the problem itself. Ethics is nothing more than the formulation of civilization's ideals; according to Freud it expresses what he calls the cultural superego. If this cultural superego formulates rules in an ethics for the purpose of preserving human community and avoiding war of all against all, then the ethics itself is a cultural phenomenon, not something which could reconcile man's cultural and natural existence. At best ethics can be regarded, following Freud, as a *therapeutic* project, which limits the harm that people cannot help but suffer as a result of the contradictions inherent in their nature and the contradictions between individual and cultural aspirations. Such a therapy, however, is about as much a path to happiness as a leg in plaster is better than an open fracture.

> The cultural super-ego [Freud writes] has developed its ideals and it formulates its demands. Amongst the latter, those concerning the relations between people are grouped together as ethics. In all eras the highest value has been placed on these ethics, as if especially great achievements have been expected of them. And ethics does, in fact, address what we can easily recognize as the sorest spot in every culture. Ethics should thus be thought of as an attempt

> at therapy, an effort to achieve via a command of the superego what has not yet been achievable through other cultural activity. As we already know, the question is how the greatest impediment to civilization - people's aggressive tendencies towards each other - can be eliminated, and this is why we are particularly interested by what is probably the most recent of the superego cultural commands, the commandment: Love thy neighbour as thyself.

Religious and philosophical ethics attempt to attain a goal which normal 'cultural activity', as Freud calls it, cannot. Normal cultural activity is the bringing up of children, and psychotherapy and philosophical ethics can be understood as a continuation or revision of this. As such it cannot step outside the culture. Religion and philosophy are themselves cultural phenomena, even when they invite us to quit civilization in favour of a so-called 'return to nature'. An ethics of strength, such as Nietzsche seems to have partly advocated, is also a cultural phenomenon, even when it appeals to nature like a Christian ethics of brotherly love. For Freud psychoanalysis, too, is a servant of civilization. Psychoanalysis and ethics sit in the same natural–cultural boat so long as both try to be therapeutic, working on the damage to lives in adults that results from their natural–cultural fragmentation. In his psychoanalysis of civilization Freud attempts to show the extent to which cultural achievements are based on a sublimation, a refusal to let one's drives run free, and how they are reliant on this and always will be. Freud hopes that one day civilization will be able to divert human drives with the least possible efforts at suppression and in the most truthful way possible. Hence his interest in Christian ethics. The commandment 'Love thy neighbour as thyself' is, for Freud, the 'strongest defence against human aggression and an excellent example of the unpsychological proceedings of the cultural superego'. And yet, Freud thinks that 'the commandment cannot be obeyed; such a huge inflation of love can only diminish its value, not eliminate the problem.'

Once people realize that there is no transcendent power which requires them to sacrifice their desires, once they realize that all civilization is mankind's doing, constructed to protect people from nature, and especially their *own* nature, then according to Freud maybe they will no longer see the civilizing mechanisms as alien forces of constraint. For as long as the process of civilization remains protected by religious illusions and philosophical quests for, and promises of, happiness, civilization itself will be threatened at the moment when these promises and deterrents are revealed as illusions. For as long as the expectations of what civilization can achieve are exaggerated, i.e., with regards to happiness or immortality, it will always be despised as something that falls short of expectations, i.e., something that has *failed*, and its claims about sublimating drives will be rejected.

'The fateful question for the human species,' Freud writes at the end of *Civilization and its Discontents*, 'seems to be whether and to what extent its cultural development will succeed in mastering the disruption of communal life by the human drives of aggression and self-destruction.'

Unhappiness, truth, beauty

With his theory of drives Freud provided a diagnosis for the complexion of organic life, albeit focusing on how it is embedded in civilization or the difficulties of integrating it into civilization. The biological determinants of life which Freud used as his starting point still come across as individual in his work. We must understand, however, that our biological life is not just an individual fact, for an essential determinant of our organic existence stems from *genes*. These genes are extraordinary objects. Although they are something very concrete in the form of DNA stored in the nuclei of our cells, as biological 'information' (a largely undefined term) they are highly abstract, almost like the types of a sign system in which the structure of our organic existence is more or less determined precisely.

The best biological theory that we have about the origins of life (and which Freud already knew, albeit not in its current form) assumes that this sign system – the overall structure as well as the concrete sequence of signs – emerged *along natural historical lines* over the course of the evolution of organic life. As individuals we neither have control over which cultural contexts we live in, nor can we decide whether or not we are born, nor do we have any influence over the structure of our own biological existence. Some people aim to compensate for this impotence with ascetic exercises in which they achieve great mastery over their body. But ultimately this is another unattainable quest for power.

Advances in reproductive medicine mean that not only can our parents determine whether we exist or not (i.e., whether they produce us or not), but also how we are created, by choosing from the fertilized egg cells those which best correspond to what they want. The structures from which they can choose are also the result of billions of years of life on our planet. From a historical perspective, therefore, our organic existence is something manifestly 'deep' and 'alien'. 'Deep' in the sense that the structure of our organism is determined by processes which, according to Stephen Jay Gould, can only be identified on the scale of deep time, i.e., they stretch back millions of years into the sphere of non-human time. It is 'alien' in the sense that it has nothing to do with our individual consciousness, nor with what we call *human* biology, and certainly not with what we call human *civilization*. From the standpoint of biological evolution, human civilization is too young to have already left behind serious traces in our genetic material.

Of course, we are not merely our organic existence, but it is *part* of what we are – here we can again concur with Freud. Compared to the history which this existence has as a genetic type, the individual history of a person's unconscious is less than a flash of lightning on the timescale. It is extremely improbable that those wishes and intentions which develop in our individual consciousness in any way 'match up' with our organic configuration. The furniture which we inherit from our grandparents does not match the tastes we have today. So why should our emotional life, drives and corporeality match what has been established in our consciousness on the basis of signs to which we are exposed during our upbringing?

Human life consists of several layers: an organic one which we cannot choose ourselves; a cultural one which our parents lay over us, which we have no authority over either, and which already represents an *attempt to inhibit* our organic dynamics; and finally the layer which develops when we begin to take responsibility for ourselves at the age of fourteen or fifteen, and try to live up to or abandon the ideals with which our parents raised us.

Let us take an image to illustrate our situation. For thousands of years a rapid river has been flowing through a valley, repeatedly uprooting trees, especially in times of heavy thawing in the mountains from where the river springs. A dam wall is built to prevent so many trees from being uprooted on the far side of the river, and to harness the water power for energy. Then we are ordered to move into an apartment in this power station, in this wall. We are worried by the rapid river and we find the wall ugly, but there is nowhere else for us to go. Although we dream of powerful rivers that do not uproot anything, and of walls that are as beautiful as soft meadows, these contradictions are only possible in dreams.

We are as little disposed to the beauty of the torrential river as the ugliness of the wall damming it. The concept of harmony, which seems to be embedded in the idea of happiness, is the concept of the reconcilability of contradictions. And yet, unsatisfied with their own lives, people see that this reconcilability does not exist. Thus images of happiness are basically not beautiful ones, because they are *untrue*. Here – if not in his assumption about the immortal soul – Plato is right that truth and beauty belong together. Thus there is *no beautiful* image of human happiness, because there is no *true image* of it. Untruth only ruins our existence even more than it is already ruined by the contradictions we have to live with. Let us forget happiness and the untrue images which have been made of it! Let us not ruin life with false claims and lies! Let us seek truth and its beauty instead of happiness! The beautiful image is a different one from that of happy people, it is *without* people and without the contradictions they embody. This was described by Ernst Jandl:

The Beautiful Picture

spare the beautiful picture from people
so you can spare yourself the tears that
everyone demands; spare it every trace of mankind:
let no path recall a sure step, no field a loaf of bread,
no forest a house and cupboard, no stone a wall,
no spring a drink, no pond no lake no sea
swimmers, boats, oars, sails, ocean voyages
no rock climbers, no cloud
people battling the weather, no piece of sky
a glance upwards, aeroplane, spaceship – let nothing
recall anything; save for white white
black black, red red, straight straight,
round round;
thus will my soul recover.

Antonio Rojaz Marten
Santiago de Chile

CHAPTER FIVE

Intensity and security as requirements of happy experiences

Notions of possible and impossible happiness

Whether happiness exists and whether we as humans can attain it depends on what we mean by 'happiness'. We can devise a concept of happiness that makes it unattainable or one that makes it very simple to achieve. But there is no point in drawing up a notion of happiness which describes something that people cannot realize. For it is quite clear that people do strive for happiness and claim, presumably not always untruthfully, that they have been happy. What would it mean if they were in pursuit of something fundamentally unachievable? Why should those who claim to be happy be labelled as hypocrites because of other people's melancholic language?

A concept either has a relevance for human action, which we can detect if possession of this concept – or the lack of it – makes a difference to a person's life, or it has no relevance and is part of the 'verbal music' which is concocted for living, but which can be ignored without anything fundamental changing in our lives. From a purely theoretical perspective there is as little evidence to prove or refute the existence of 'happiness' as of 'God'. We need to ask what human life would look like without this or that concept of God or happiness; and to get a clear view of them we need to identify the function these concepts have in people's actions.

Illusions and the notions associated with them no doubt play an important role in human life, too. The illusion of a paradise, for example, which some Muslims believe is attainable after death, may drive a suicide bomber to carry out an attack. Without such a concept of paradise as a resting place for their soul after death, they may not have committed the murderous deed. It might be possible to devise a concept of 'happiness' that works in a similar way to that of paradise, i.e., it is an illusory concept and yet has a function in human life. It is not possible to conceive of paradise as the location of the soul after death in such a way that it represents either an illusion or something real, because it *always* refers to a hope, either an illusory one or one which comes true for all of us. Besides this hope, however, it never refers to something which would determine the way we act *now* (for we cannot verify if the way we act will have a successful outcome for the soul after death, nor do we know anything about taking action in the places where the soul supposedly resides after death). While talk of the soul in paradise only ever refers to a possibility, that of happiness is sometimes based on hopes and illusions, and sometimes on the reality of the present. Thus the concept of happiness as an eternal state of the soul in contemplation of God following its release from the body is merely hypothetical and probably illusory. I will not pursue this concept any further, even though the illusion has consequences for human behaviour, and was particularly significant in the past when the Christian churches promised salvation and happiness in the afterlife if people lived their lives in a particular way. Instead I will work solely with the assumption that real pain, actual suffering and conflict are factors which are usually *absent* in those moments when people say they are happy.

People generally use the term 'happiness' to describe a pleasant, enjoyable and intense state of mind, for example when they talk about the 'happiness of love', or say that an aesthetic experience such as going to a concert or reading a book made them happy for a while. It is a state of mind which people arrive at when they are broadly in harmony with themselves and others around them, when the things they are involved with do not impede, disturb or harm them, but also when they are conscious of intense experiences, like the sportsperson who is feted as the victor after a hard contest and describes themselves as happy. They have survived the conflict and their success is acknowledged by other people.

Such a state of happiness is not simply one of freedom from pain. If that were true then death or unconsciousness would also be states of happiness. It does not materialize without a certain intensity of experience, which people call 'happiness'. The *specific relationship* between intensity and freedom from conflict which must exist for the person to be able to call themselves happy must not be banal, trivial or boring, nor must it be so extremely tense that the person feels threatened. Reference was once made – in the context of ethics and the difficulty of their expression – to a feeling that 'nothing could happen' to you. We can also use this expression to describe the experience of happiness: a feeling that nothing threatening could happen to you; that you are in the right place ('safe and sound'); that you belong where you are; and that you observe with great attention and pleasure how you yourself and the world you inhabit at that moment are constituted.

This balance between *intensity and serenity* in an experience, between the rich contrasts of the experience and the lack of threat to one's existence may be different for each person. For example, a mountain hike may produce this very balance in an experienced hiker, but represent a threat to another, inexperienced person who feels vertigo when looking down from a great height. For a child a cartoon may offer precisely the right relationship between excitement and feelings of security, whereas an adult may find it lacks intensity and become bored. This means that happiness, as an intense and contrast-rich, but unthreatening and generally conflict-free experience, can be of varying degrees, both relative to the person experiencing the situation and from situation to situation. Because different people have different needs vis-à-vis intensity and differing abilities to overcome conflict their judgements of different experiences will vary in the degree of happiness these represent.

All these interpretations are no more than suggestions. Because everybody at some point in their life experiences intense but unthreatening situations, everybody can relate to something from amongst these suggestions of how we might be happy. The intention here is not to provide a clear-cut definition of happiness from which – as philosophers love to do these days – criteria can be inferred as to when an experience is happy and when not. Nobody sets criteria and uses them to check whether they are happy or not at that very moment, just as nobody would draw up a concept of 'full', infer from this criteria of 'fullness' and after a good meal analyse whether their own state fulfilled these criteria or not. Only a few philosophical pedants would question the remark 'God, I'm happy' by suggesting that certain criteria should be applied to check the nature of the experience of the person uttering this remark, and to verify whether that person is *justified* in making such an exclamation. Our focus here is not outlandish justifications of linguistic usage but simply to form a concept of happiness that corresponds to our experience, analyses it and articulates the fact that happiness may be rare but it is possible. From this finding the intention is to discover *when* it is possible and to what extent its possibility *depends on us*.

At certain stages of development in our lives we can all imagine constellations of experience which give rise to the feeling of being happy. But the fact that these constellations are conceivable does not mean that they necessarily occur or that we can *induce* them. Because people always live in complex social situations in which they themselves are changed and which they change through their actions, the precarious balance between intensity and freedom from conflict, which the experience of happiness makes possible, is something of a rarity in the flux of life, and usually vanishes again after a short while. Analyses of happiness, however, often severely underestimate the complexities in which people find themselves at certain periods of their lives.

People and things

The first complexity we need to address, and one which is usually ignored, is the relationship between people and things. People and things enter a variety of relationships and mutually influence each other in a way which is crucial for happiness. It would be false to assume that people have a fixed subjective nature, things a fixed objective structure and that when the two meet this produces certain experiences. The thinking of the past century has repeatedly shown that this juxtaposition of a rigid subjectivity and a fixed objectivity is wrong. The following view was already being espoused by Ernst Cassirer at the beginning of the twentieth century:

> Initially people do not have a fixed idea of subject and object, according to which they adjust their behaviour; but in the whole of this behaviour, in all their physical and spiritual-mental activities they start with the knowledge of both, it is the horizon of the I which first parts ways with that of reality. From the start there is not a fixed, static relationship between the two, but a fluctuating movement, as it were, that goes back and forth – and this gradually produces the form in which people understand their own existence as well as that of objects.

As simple as this idea appears, it is a far-reaching one. First we must note that people who develop in different material environments become different people, or people of different 'forms' as Cassirer puts it. A person growing up in a world of straw huts, spears, arrows and canoes, etc., will become a different person from one who is raised in a world of skyscrapers, cars, aeroplanes, computers and telephones, etc. We would normally say that it is the different *social* relations in the different societies where these things exist that result in the variety of people around the world. That is surely correct, but it is not the whole truth.

Interaction with different things demands and fosters different habits and skills, leads to specific ways of perceiving and moving, different chains of association and fantasies. Just as there are constellations of mutual influence between people, there are constellations of mutual change between people and things, which, as with the constellations between people, lead to experiences that can be *evaluated*. If we imagine a person who has grown up amongst straw huts, spears and canoes trying to live in a city in all likelihood they will be unhappy, because the structure of their subjectivity does not match the things they now suddenly find around them. Situations like these are depicted in the film *Dersu Uzala* by Akira Kurosawa. The Russian soldiers from the city who have come to survey the largely uncultivated land in Siberia are 'out of place' on the steppe, and Uzala the tribesman, who befriends the captain of the expeditionary troop and follows him back to the city, finds himself out of place, too. He discovers he cannot spend the whole day sitting in a 'stone tomb', as the houses seem to him, and his habit of hunting with his rifle goes to waste in a place where people survive by purchasing food in shops with money. The things that Uzala is used to experiencing and doing bear no relation to the place where he finds himself at the end of the film or to the things that surround him. This is why he is unhappy.

Many older people must have similar experiences. Their material environment changes, and those that change it often think they are making old people's lives easier by providing them with a food processor, computer or DVD player. But the experiences and behaviour older people are used to are perhaps not adapted to these things, which means that rather than their lives being made easier, they are permanently required to change and adapt. What these things always highlight is that the older people's subjectivity does not fit in with that world of things which other people judge to be practical and interesting.

People take basic pleasure in perception and purposeful action. But their habits of perceiving and acting, and those skills associated with these habits are always related to certain constellations of things that more or less 'fit' with the schemes of perceiving and acting. For example, Uzala can read a tiger's tracks; he can pursue a deer; he can build a shelter out of steppe grass. He cannot play music on the violin – his ear has not been accustomed to European classical music; he cannot read novels and cannot compare prices in a shop, etc. This is why his habits of perception and action go to waste in the city, and he lacks those he needs in the material contexts of the city. This fact – that there is no fit between subjective skills and the world – leads to *experiences of alienation*.

Feeling alienated is often described as an unhappy experience, and the alienation is not only an alien environment, an alien language and alien social customs, but also an alien world of things. The discrepancy between a *new* world of things and the structure of subjectivity acquired in the past is often regarded, if not as unhappiness – and certainly not as happiness – then as alienation engendered by the 'new times' and conflict-laden. It is true that people themselves have created things such as rifles and computers, straw huts and canoes. But the fact that these objects are technological creations *by* people does not mean that all things made by people suit *all* people in all times. The home, too, and the familiar surroundings of external life in which we have accommodated ourselves by developing specific habits, always form a context of things. Truculent objects play a key role in many clown sketches: the paper which cannot be shaken off the hand; the board which hits the head of another clown each time the one carrying it moves; the hosepipe which either refuses to spurt water or does so at the wrong time and out of holes it was not meant to, etc. It is not only human clumsiness which is being depicted here, but also the autonomy of things. Although our habits are oriented to them, they do not always obey these habits, nor are they totally controlled by them.

It is not only clown sketches that reveal the absurdities that result when things do not behave as planned. Things that are there even though they should not be – like a stone blocking the road – or which are not there, even though they should be – such as the missing key at the bottom of the handbag – can be troublesome or even trigger catastrophes, like the leaking rubber rings on the fuel tanks of the *Challenger* space shuttle, which – unlike the garden hose with the holes in the wrong place – are not a joke.

When considering the compatibility between humans and non-human things, like most living entities people always focus on things that can be eaten. Evidently there are inclinations and aversions to certain foods, which are independent of our habit forming, for example when children want to scoff everything that is sweet, but reject anything that is bitter. Later on in life things are produced and prepared by eaters in highly cultivated and technological ways so that they can serve as food. There is a food industry just as there is a car industry and there are restaurant critics who report on fancy restaurants just as there are art critics.

People are not so selective with – or as thorough in their evaluation of – other things. Far less consideration is given to the sights and sounds we might wish to experience than to the question of food. Even though other senses can evaluate phenomena in the same way that taste can, for example by classifying things as 'noise' and 'euphony' or 'a beautiful view' and 'a horrible view', people rarely think about the consequences of experiencing certain sights or sounds. The fact that it is (allegedly) bad for us to eat cake all the time, drink alcohol and smoke is not perceived on the same level as the fact that most people do not enjoy looking at a weather-beaten wall or listening to construction noise. Do other things have an equivalent to 'poisoning' from tainted food? Are we 'harmed' by a 'bad' building if we live in it? There is no doubt that permanent construction noise can make you unwell and that the changing pictures on the television will probably leave behind some trace in the brain, just as changing meals leave a trace in our organism, leading to the adaptation of our digestive and detoxification systems. It is pretty certain, in view of the continuities which exist between an organism and its environment, that things have many more effects than merely those which are a result of food intake. There is probably more happening here than we have been able to know and analyse up till now, because we have not yet carried out enough detailed research into the interaction between our bodies and things.

We cannot simply describe the process of scientific understanding and its technological application in what is called the 'modern era' since 1600 as one in which people have increasingly acquired *greater power* over – and *independence* from – natural circumstances and coincidences by creating artificial things and controlling the spaces we inhabit; such as our independence from wind and water power by the invention of machines powered by coal or uranium, or our substantial independence from the weather by the creation of artificial living spaces in cities. What has also happened, in fact, is that increasingly more *connections* and *dependencies* between things and 'us' and the consequences of 'our' actions on the world of things have become apparent. This has given rise to a stronger consciousness of 'our' entanglement with the world of things and a growing obligation to be careful with the way 'we' act, because the network of consequences of our actions is perceived as something which is becoming increasingly tight-knit. The eating and digestion of food, which can also be described as a transformation of industrially designed things (i.e., foodstuffs), is only the tip of an iceberg of adjustments, constructions and reconstructions which take place between people and things, partly consciously and deliberately, partly unconsciously and apparently without any goal.

Adjustments

If adjustments are fuelled by conflict and threat, the unadjusted state is one in which happy experiences are unlikely because we still need to change ourselves or the world. Aspects of this task may make us happy because it develops skills and can have a successful outcome. And yet the state of happiness is more likely to come about via established habits, so that we change ourselves and the world of things in a way which makes us feel that we fit in with the world, live in the right place and in the right circumstances. People who have consciously sought happiness have always thought very precisely about not only what they should eat, but also in what sort of environment they need to live, and how the natural things and artificially manufactured objects around them should be ordered to enable them to achieve happiness. In recent times the complex connection between people and things of natural and technical origin has been regarded (by Bruno Latour, following Whitehead's concept of 'society') as a *hybrid collective*.

What is important about this notion is that the human, natural and technological cannot be separated. Rather they have a constant effect on each other and none of them can be changed without the others changing, too. The idea of something 'purely' human, independent of nature and technology, is the same abstraction as the idea that nature and technology are independent of each other and of mankind. As a rule, the use of these abstractions has only an ideological function, if 'nature' has to be 'saved' or 'protected' from 'mankind' or 'technology', or if we want to use 'technology' to make ourselves secure from the 'natural elements', or if we think we need to preserve 'what is human' from technology or natural brutalization.

Today, for example, there is scarcely a human brain on the planet which is not structured by technology, and here I do not necessarily mean the technology of psychopharmacology (although it will probably increase in importance), but media technology which turns our brains into ones which allow us to watch television, telephone and use computers. One muscle might be used to lift heavy weights or hold onto something for a length of time, whereas another moves only light loads and needs to hold onto things only for a short time. In the same way, a brain which is used to process a rapid succession of images and operate a keyboard is different from one which does not come into contact with these things.

On the other hand, all technology is the applied knowledge of natural relations and a continuation of natural developments by human beings. For humans, nature is something that threatens us, or which we think we have to fit in with or change, because otherwise it might destroy us; or nature seems to be something beneficial which sustains us. *Everything* human is a hybrid of nature and technology, in which the natural, the technological and the human become indistinguishable, because all people act and get used to acting *in a certain way*, and these ways of acting are nothing more than adaptation techniques, techniques of shaping ourselves and the world. The muscle of a photographic model, toughened and 'honed' in the gym – what is it? Something natural? Definitely, because it would not be as it is if the natural evolution of mammals had not taken place. Is it something technological? Definitely, because the machines which the photographic model works out on have been designed to train and form muscles in a particular way. Is it something human and cultural? Certainly, because it is, after all, part of a human being who earns their money in a human culture by embodying a particular ideal of beauty. Regarding the question of whether happiness is possible, however, what is most important about these formation processes in which the natural, technological and human are inextricably linked, is their *temporal* structure.

At the right and wrong time

If we have dashed to get to the station on time, but our train has a three-hour delay, we get annoyed. We adjusted ourselves to the timetable, but the train company failed to stick to the timetable. If there is no rain in spring after sowing and the seeds do not germinate, the farmer is in trouble, as is maybe the population dependent on the grain for food. If a mother dies in childbirth and cannot nurse and bring up her child, the relatives are sad. Infuriation, trouble and grief are not compatible with happiness. In all these cases feelings of unhappiness develop (to use a rather strong expression for the first, but not second and third examples) because the temporal sequences do not match. I ran for the train, but the train *did not stick to the timetable* and is not there yet. The farmer planted the seeds, but the rain which should germinate them does not come *at the anticipated or right time*. The mother has carried the child in pregnancy, but dies *prematurely* in childbirth.

The causal complexity in which people are bound up with technological and natural things is one of *happenings or events* in procedures and synchronicities. Evaluating whether things fit or do not fit is not merely a question of whether schemes of perception and action can be applied to certain things, but also whether procedures take place in the 'right' sequence and at the right speed, and whether planned synchronicities can be achieved. If the migratory birds fly north in 'anticipation' of the spring, but spring does not arrive, then a synchronicity fails to happen, just as with the train that fails to arrive.

Anticipated procedures and synchronicities and actual procedures and synchronicities are not bound to the differentiation between the natural, technological and human, either. We could also describe the hybrid collectives as *pulsating*, in which patterns of natural, technological and individual sequences and synchronicities are created, partly by human activity, such as the train timetable, and partly independently, such as the seasons. Experiences of conflict and experiences of 'matches' are always related to such sequences and synchronicities. The colours in a picture are synchronous; the notes in a melody are perceived as a sequence. Meeting a friend unexpectedly in the market square is a 'happy' synchronicity; being struck by lightning an unhappy one. An error-free logical proof is a successful sequence; an array of technical faults and human errors, such as what happened in the Chernobyl reactor accident, is a disastrous sequence.

If something happens at the same time as something else or in a particular sequence it acquires a *meaning*, and for the observers and those concerned a *value*. The fact that something 'fits in with' something else, as it says in some accounts, that someone meets the 'right' people at the 'right' time so that the information they can be given is relevant to them, is an example of happiness in the sense of a coincidence. Happiness in life is not independent of happy coincidence.

It is conceivable that a person has all the potential to be able to enjoy experiences of great intensity in the sense outlined above. Let us assume that someone has trained to become a great musician and this talent could make them happy. But then war breaks out or a natural catastrophe occurs. Now they cannot realize their potential, for wars or earthquakes cause the world in which playing music is of relevance to disappear. If that person had been born thirty years earlier or later and had undergone the same training, their talent would have been a source of happiness. Because of the synchronicities over which they have no influence, however, it becomes worthless. People who have to live through a war or a major natural catastrophe sometimes say with justification that they were 'born at the wrong time': 'Insistence on birth at the wrong season is the trick of evil.'

If people adapt themselves to given circumstances or adapt the circumstances to their attributes, this process of adjustment needs time. As we have already noted, the process of adaptation itself is seldom something which is perceived by those who adapt or adapt things to themselves as a happy experience. So when people adapt in order for their habits to fit in with the world, they usually pay a price: in the most trivial cases this is a hard struggle and discomfort; in the worst instances the price is pain. Because our lifetimes are finite and adaptation processes are seldom happy experiences, the expenditure of portions of our lifetime can be seen as a price in itself. These days, for example, many people who use a computer wonder whether they should learn to use a new programme, i.e., adapt to a new machine, or whether the time and discomfort this involves is just too high a price to pay for the promise touted by those selling the new programme that it will make our work easier. Moreover, the schedule of our activity may be organized in a way that makes sense only when one task follows on from another in a particular sequence, such as in a production process based on the division of labour. If something is changed at any point in this process, the entire temporal structure of the process can go awry.

Threats to identity

People know who they are and what their world is, because their habits fit in with the world around them. This does not always necessarily go hand in hand with contrast-rich experiences and a sense of security, i.e., happiness. Viewed simply, it merely means that they are not strangers to themselves or the world. The ability to endure experiences of alienation and to adapt to new circumstances even after childhood is a useful one which is valued positively. If, however, the dynamic of world change on the one hand, and the high regard for human flexibility on the other mean that people are *permanently* changing, *forever* producing new patterns of habits, and that while developing new patterns of habits they have to face the fact that the things to which they are trying to adapt at any given time are already vanishing again, then they slip into a maelstrom of change which threatens what has been designated as their 'identity'. Then people stop knowing who they are and in what sort of world they actually live. The world of modern capitalism has been described as one which results in phenomena of total flexibilization and threats to identity. By the yardstick of our concept of happiness, such circumstances are apt to make people unhappy.

For if people, on the basis of particular identities, plan out their lives and try to organize the world according to these plans, the upheavals of identity formation and preservation make such planning difficult or even impossible. If we regard everything that happens independently of our plans as subjectively coincidental or inevitable, coincidence becomes increasingly important in a world which makes people so mutable that they can scarcely plan anything any longer. At the same time, a willingness to take risks becomes an increasingly valuable human trait, and the inclination to get involved in processes, which are only partly controllable through planning and whose speed and complexity make their outcome highly unpredictable, increases in importance. In these circumstances flexibility and willingness to take risks replace experience and level-headedness as virtues. For past experiences are worthless in rapidly changing situations, and the inclination to make detailed plans is less relevant where it is assumed that processes cannot essentially be planned, but rather we need to react situationally to coincidences. In these circumstances people become unhappy if they seek a security in planning their lives which allows them to enjoy intense experiences without threat. If people abandon life-planning they still may enjoy intense experiences in unthreatening contexts. But then the feeling of security needs to come from another source than a faith in the ability to live according to one's life plan.

A popular option here is *celebration* and *ecstasy*. Human beings have always created social and physical structures in which they can remove themselves from the so-called everyday conditions of life and focus for a defined period of time on intensifying their experience in secure conditions. These secure conditions are *exceptional circumstances*, however: those of the celebration. When life plans become pointless, the ecstasy which a celebration – but not only a celebration – can engender becomes more significant. The same view claims that the intensity of ecstasy can replace the intense experience of contextual relations, which could also be described as *meaning*. The increase in the pursuit of intensity through ecstasy could also, if this diagnosis is correct, be a symptom of the fact we are experiencing ever fewer meaningful contexts of the sort established by our life plans. And yet ecstasy seems to offer the same possibility of experiencing happiness as the feeling that suddenly everything fits into a plan, as the intensity of a meaningful context at a particular moment in life where no apparent threat is present. If a moment appears as the culmination of a plan – for example somebody plans to carry out a specific task and realizes at a specific moment that it will succeed – then the certainty of the plan's success and the intensity of the 'reflection' of a temporal whole in a momentary part produces the conditions for experiencing happiness, without having to take a 'time-out' from life which the state of ecstasy represents. In this case the experience of happiness is something which occurs in the course of life, whereas the state of ecstasy occurs in a 'time-out' or a 'holiday from life', as Robert Musil called it.

There is no reason, however, to label the experience of happiness in the course of life as the *true* or *real* one as opposed to a *false* or *unreal* experience of happiness brought on through ecstasy. The happiness that can develop in celebratory states of ecstasy has been criticized because its after-effects sometimes impair the ability to stick to life plans, or because occasionally it produces a dependency on the 'exceptional circumstances', an addiction to the ecstasy. This view is only sustainable, however, for as long as identities and larger life contexts continue to feature as elements of social systems. In a completely dynamized world of flexible people without lasting identities of habit patterns, a strict delineation between everyday, planned time and celebration as the exception is no longer possible because the significance of coincidence and the change in life circumstances also turn normal life into a sort of 'ecstatic frenzy'. Even if the intensity of the celebration does not predominate on a permanent basis, there is an ever-recurring 'exhilaration of change', which arises when people move from one place to the next and from one narrow social context of a partner, friends and neighbours to the next, without being able or wanting to maintain links with what has gone before in the sense of preserving one's identity.

The flip side of 'exhilaration of change' is the fear of unfamiliarity of new situations, which is more likely if the new situation appears to be *more threatening* than the previous one. Getting to know other people takes time, and it takes even more time to develop a common pattern of habits with other people to produce a relatively conflict-free co-existence. People who do not have the time to embark on such a process of familiarization with each other have to forgo the feeling of security imparted by narrow ties with shared habits, and satisfy themselves with a certain superficiality or 'outsider's view' on the lives of others and a corresponding insecurity vis-à-vis relationships. 'Fear of the unfamiliar' – the strongest emotional state which can be projected onto other people from an external perspective – is a feeling which is not only associated with the fear of conflict that potentially arises from incompatible living habits, but also one which results from the fear of having to get involved in a struggle – a struggle to understand as well as a struggle to adapt to what you have understood. If the constellations between people change again, before a potential process of mutual adjustment and habit-forming can be concluded, the usual outcome is social disorientation. It is similar with the relationship between people and things. It takes time to adapt to things, whether we are talking about the furniture in new surroundings or learning how to using technical equipment such as cars or computers. If things change more rapidly than people can adapt to them and learn how to work with and operate them, the result will also be disorientation in the world of things.

In societies with scientific–technological systems a high value is placed on progress. A greater price is placed on yielding new knowledge than on producing certainties. The manufacture of technological devices is also linked to a market in which a premium is placed on the rapid turnover of newer and newer goods, because higher profits can be achieved in a shorter time. As things produced technologically are an essential part of the human world, an acceleration in the collective production of knowledge and its technological application is leading to an increasingly rapid change in the world of things and human habits related to these.

This process of acceleration takes no account of the limits governing people's ability to adapt, form habits and successfully complete learning processes. Nor does it take account of the fact that people's flexibility and capacity to learn usually declines in certain areas as they get older, which means they always need more time to form new habits. In such a world the rigidity of old people's habit patterns and identities tend to be viewed negatively, interpreted as dated inflexibility. It no longer holds true that young people are the ones who have not yet adapted to the world in contrast to older people who have been on this earth for a long time and have become attuned to it. In fact, as flexible beings from the start, young people are able to jump aboard the permanently changing world almost at will and take on the risk of having their own identity (if this exists) turned inside out. Older people, on the other hand, either just drop out of the process of continual world change or they are jettisoned from it, as participants in technological production, for example.

This seriously reduces the possibility of the elderly sharing happiness with young people, because in social systems that are structured in such a way different generations find it easy to withdraw into different worlds of things and communities. The elderly can only preserve their identity if they isolate their social and material world from the accelerated processes of change. It is perfectly possible to isolate oneself in such a way and not only as a reaction to the most recent dynamization of life circumstances. Monasteries and communities of 'drop-outs' have always represented spaces of isolated and fixed social and material circumstances. In these communities that have broken out of the processes of acceleration, happiness is less subject to chance than in the patterns of life circumstances which are pulsating at a higher frequency and accelerating all the time, and which are a result of the interlinking of scientific–technological progress with capitalist markets. Here 'nature' appears frequently because the changes are generally slow and the rhythms which recur – ignoring catastrophes such as earthquakes, volcanic eruptions and meteorite impacts – represent a counter-world of calm, which, to those who do not seek their experiences of happiness in the contingencies of flexibility, appear more secure than the scientifically–technologically manufactured world of things. All talk of the 'naturalness' of the 'simple' and 'slow' life and the 'unnaturalness' of the dynamized life circumstances in the scientifically–technologically created world of capitalist markets ignores the fact that the progress-focused 'momentum' of scientific research and technology and turnover of goods is also something 'natural' in the sense that no human beings are steering it. At most we have commentators providing positive and critical reactions to processes which are developing of their own accord. Neither natural nor social processes have been designed by some mind *for people*. It would be a mistake, however, to assume that, where there are no circumstances *created* specifically for human ideas, experiences of happiness are impossible. The creation of things and circumstances always begins with the identities which exist *prior to* the process of *design*. And yet the process of *design* changes those creating it as well as the things and circumstances which were created for them. Because of this feedback, planning can never guarantee a match between people and people, and people and things.

Just as two people who meet and get together because they like each other, change each other mutually by being together – possibly to the extent that they no longer like each other – people can create certain things which because of their identity at the time of creation seem very helpful, but which repel them after a certain adaptation to these objects. There are always people who say that they really liked this car, this computer, this house at the moment they imagined them or saw them from the outside. But when they realized what these things got up to with their habits of moving, writing or living, they felt repelled by them. Such opinions are generally expressed by older people who have fixed habits in these areas before adapting to the new things. It is a very different picture for children who grow up with those same things and acquire their first habits through them. Take an older person who, over the course of several decades, has got used to travelling by train, writing in ink and living in an apartment. If, after getting used to driving a car, writing with a computer and living in a house, they find they have not adapted to a more pleasant world but have simply become a different person who no longer plans journeys, has any regard for smooth paper and dark ink or talks to their neighbours, then within this person a *contrast* has developed between the person they remember in the past and the one they are observing in the present. It is only when such a contrast reveals the change in our own person that we can also see how much things, like other people, influence us. Just as the mere compatibility of two people with such and such personalities is unlikely to lead to happiness, because people are constantly changing as a result of their mutual contact – their being together is a process and, at best, experiences of happiness can occur within this personal process of change – so happiness cannot arise from total adaptation to the perfect world of things, i.e., one which eliminates all unpleasant experiences, because people and things change as a result of mutual interaction. The assumption of static, compatible relationships is probably a basic error of concepts of happiness based on technological progress.

In fact, these deliberations present a very elementary challenge to the idea of adaptation. If happiness is regarded as the result of the adaptation of the world to humans or of humans to the world, this view generally conceals the procedural entanglement of both sides brought about by processes of change with uncertain outcomes *prior to* these adaptations. Such entanglement leads to mutual and only slightly predictable change, which can interfere with the *planned* adaptations. People adapt to the climate by using heating, and with the heating they change the climate. The fact that the climate is changing in turn changes the people who come up with other ideas for generating a temperature that is comfortable to them, etc. *All* processes in hybrid collectives of people and things run according to this pattern.

Given the knowledge of this dynamic, happiness is only impossible if it is regarded as the result of successful adaptation. If, on the other hand, happiness is understood to be what *appears* when intense experiences in unthreatening contexts become possible, happiness is not completely independent from adaptation processes if successful adaptation generally results in a certain security, i.e., the interaction of people with each other and things that leads to a certain stability of circumstances. But this security is not sufficient to ensure happiness. For intense experience, which is the predominant feature of happiness, comes about unexpectedly and cannot be planned. Some hymnal poems document the intense experience of 'belonging', of this thing or this being producing a feeling of joy in the world, the experience that this is not the result of having to dress up one's own mind or the world, but something akin to an *epiphany* in a happy moment. In this respect experiences of happiness in relatively unthreatening circumstances are certainly possible, but unlike secure circumstances, they cannot be planned. Although experiences of happiness are partly down to us, they are not something we can *produce* in every way by changing ourselves, other people or the things around us.

James Williamson
Grantchester/Cambridge

CHAPTER SIX

Polyphony

'The Tathāgata has done away with all opinions'
Buddha

The death of Stanley Low

We cannot be sure if he anticipated his death or planned it, whether it was an accident or a suicide he had contemplated for a long time. After having finished his corrections to the proofs of this book on a Friday, Stanley Low flew from Hanover to Zurich at lunchtime to visit his daughter and ex-wife. His ex-wife later said that Low had left the house on the Zürichberg after a row with his thirteen-year-old daughter that afternoon. The life insurance company's inquiry ascertained that he took a taxi from Spyriplatz, directly below the family apartment, and drove to the Garnerland, where he stayed the night in a hotel in Elm. As the manageress said, he set out the following morning – Saturday – for a hike up the Freiberg.

Low had once told me of the mountain hikes he used to take with his daughter in the Freiberg area. They had often stopped by the last farmhouse on the Ober Ämpächli pasture, just before the Kärpf wildlife conservation area, and watched marmots through binoculars. Low said that the upright posture of these sentry animals which stand on a high point and whistle the moment a shadow passes over them, sending all the grazing members of the troop back into their burrows, led him to believe that the upright gait of human beings was a permanent sentry position. Philosophers have always attached great importance to the upright stance of humans, using it as a criterion to differentiate people from animals; for example, Plato's definition of human beings as 'featherless bipeds'. According to later philosophers, Low said, the upright stance had 'freed up the hands', supposedly allowing us to evolve and use tools, which in turn led to a rapid development of the brain and mental capacities. But apes such as baboons, who have never walked on two legs, not even for a few moments, also *sit down* so that they can use their free hands in all sorts of ways, as Low was told by the Mainz biologist, Henke. We all know this from visiting the zoo. The theory of the upright stance, which Low said was based on outdated biological theories, probably bore little relation to reality, like many philosophical narratives, he added. But Low thought that the unrestrained vanity of human beings meant that they were obsessed by the need to differentiate themselves from the animals as a species, and a number of philosophers exploited this – as did theologians, of course – to come up with some sort of 'theory of uniqueness', as it is called in anthropology.

Low himself was convinced by the continuity between people and animals. He cited Peirce's metaphysics of evolution with its synechism and Schopenhauer's theory of universal will in nature to support his conviction that human beings were animals, too, although 'unsuccessful' in a specific way, and thus unhappy, as he was wont to say. On several occasions I heard him criticize Heidegger, who claimed that human beings *died*, whereas animals *perished*; humans interpreted the *world* they lived in, whereas animals had only an *environment*. According to Low this is where Heidegger's philosophy, which he regarded as one of the most overrated of the twentieth century, reached a sad climax of nonsense, dressed-up with elaborate terminology and founded on religious prejudice.

Like Low, I believe that the continuity between humans and animals is greater than philosophers generally admit, but unlike Low I think that the categories 'happiness' and 'unhappiness' have nothing to do with *natural history*, and that it is pointless to investigate the happiness or unhappiness of tigers in relation to that of humans. It is only possible to describe animals or humans as 'successes' or 'failures' in technomorphic and theological contexts, in which we can ask whether a creator has managed to achieve their original intentions when creating the living beings. But as soon as we admit that nobody planned us or tigers or any other animal you care to mention, it becomes pointless to talk of the success or failure of one or other species. It is unlikely that animals think about their life or take pleasure in the meaning it supposedly has. If the pleasure engendered by meaningful contexts equates to happiness (and for me, at least, this is *one* plausible interpretation of the word), then they do not experience happiness. And yet I have often seen animals – dogs or monkeys for example – utterly absorbed in perception, and from the outside it looked as if these creatures were in a state of mind in which we humans feel that everything has slotted together and that we ourselves are secure in this wholeness.

Low once told me, while discussing marmots on the Freiberg, that the upright stance of humans not only made him think of the marmots' sentry position, but also of bears in *aggressive* mode, when they likewise stand up on two legs. Dogs and horses, too, threaten when in conflict by standing on their hind legs. They snap with their mouths close to their opponents' heads, so that the gnashing of their jaws can be heard. Is it not likely, Low pondered, that people move around this world on two legs because they are permanently *on guard*, permanently *threatening*, or a mixture of the two? Are not fear and aggression the basis for almost all human activity, Low wondered, especially for technology, which is so highly esteemed by philosophical anthropologists and which is primarily weapons and war technology? Seeing the enemy upright on two legs and threatening him in the same manner was probably the starting point for the upright stance of humans, he concluded.

Assuming he set off briskly that Saturday morning, Low must have passed the marmots around nine o'clock and climbed up further into the Kärpf wildlife conservation area. He could have come across ibex and chamois when he must have tried, to the north-east of the Chüebodensee and before the Wildmadfurggeli, to scale a sheer rock face. He did not have a climbing rope, hook or carabiner, not that he would have had a clue how to use these. He had no equipment at all. Not even a rucksack with a few provisions was found with his body. He was not wearing an all-weather jacket or walking shoes, but a woollen suit and his usual black Oxfords.

It was apparently drizzling in Glarus Canton that morning, so the stones must have been slippery. He fell from this rock face one hundred metres to his death. It remains unclear where he was trying to get to by climbing. There is no path directly above the rock face. All he could have reached in May was a large, fairly steep field crusted with snow, which would have been almost impossible to ascend without the right equipment, such as climbing boots and an ice pick. Maybe Low thought it was a risky climb and much too difficult for him in his Oxfords, and thus had factored in his fall and possible death – for which he had to reach a certain height. The line between accidental death and suicide only appears to be a clear one. People whose will to live is at an end often run risks, because they are no longer terrified by the danger of having an accident. Perhaps this was the case with Low. It may well be that the potentially fatal slippery rock face was what attracted him, just as some people are attracted by a deep abyss. Perhaps Low did try his best to scale the rock, but thought that the result would either be a nice view of the Chüebodensee or death, depending on how his strength and dexterity fared at this wet spot from where ledges jutted out sharply. Perhaps his intention was to jump from the snowy field and he simply slipped before getting there.

The manageress of the hotel alerted the mountain rescue service that same evening, because Low had not come back as he said he would when he set off. But there was nothing the mountain rescue service could do in the dark. On Sunday afternoon Low was found by another mountain-hiker coming down from the Wildmadfurggeli. For the relatives – especially his daughter, who last saw her father in the heat of an argument – and as far as the insurance payout was concerned, an accident was preferable to a verifiable suicide. Low did not jump from the mountain, said the experienced hiker who found him.

A picture

Low was found by a young, unusually clever young man by the name of Said Aitmatov, who had moved to Switzerland from Kyrgyzstan. I met him for the first time in Elm. As always when hiking on his own, Said had been carrying a mobile phone, one of those you can take photographs with. After spending a while at the spot and having an experience he later described to me, he took a picture of the dead Low. As he told me in his accent-free German during our meeting, he had two reasons for doing this. First, he wanted to provide some sort of documentary evidence of the accident which might prove useful later (he was right in this). Second, this young, obviously wealthy man was a painter and devoted himself with great intensity to his art, in addition to exploring the natural world, which, as I learned from conversations we had later, he had undertaken in all parts of the world, always travelling long distances on foot. It was probably his artistic impulse which gave him the urge on that occasion to capture the scree field with the dead body in a picture.

Said Aitmatov described to me how, when seeing Low's face amongst the stones on the scree field where he had fallen, he was immediately seized by a feeling which was both shocking and thrilling. It forced him to sit on a rock, where he must have stayed absolutely motionless for a period of time he could not determine. He did not know, he said, how long he had sat there. It was only when he got up again from the rock that he noticed two mountain jackdaws sitting beside him.

Low had grey hair and his face had also taken on a grey hue. As Aitmatov said, he was dressed in his green suit with its black-and-white, salt-and-pepper pattern, and wearing black shoes. (I had often seen him dressed like this at the Academy.) Low was lying between the greyish-black stones of the scree field, some of which had green-and-white patches of lichen. Just like the dead man, these stones had once fallen from the rock face, their eyes staring up at the sky and a smile on their faces. At least that is how it had seemed to Aitmatov. It was, he said, as if the dead man *belonged* there, as if he had always been lying there, or as if he had finally arrived where he had always rightly wanted to get to. There was no blood to be seen, the body was not twisted, but lay with its arms and legs outstretched like someone stretching their limbs in bed after a restful sleep. No birds or whistling marmots disturbed the stillness; it was so quiet that you could hear the sound the gentle drizzle made on the stones, according to the young mountain-climber.

He had never seen a more beautiful scree field in his life than this one with Low's dead body. As strange as it might sound, he was struck by a distressing euphoria – a feeling totally unknown to him – when he saw this smiling corpse amongst the stones, small drops of drizzle running down the man's relaxed face as if in a tender gesture. The euphoria that gripped him at the sight of the corpse was followed by an 'echo' of this feeling which went on for days. It was not as intense as the sensation – if we can call it that – which compelled him to sit on a rock and stay there in that Alpine scenery, Aitmatov said. But the emotional reverberation was a feeling he had never experienced before, either. In this mental state, visual impressions, feelings and moods entered his mind that he had not experienced since childhood, making him very cheerful. When he regained his senses on the rock by the scree field, when a sense of time returned, he remembered the mobile phone in his rucksack and took photographs of Low lying prostrate amongst the stones and of the rock face. The pictures he took back then remained imprinted on his mind until eventually he decided to paint what he had seen.

He said he was still trying to translate the scree field with Low to the canvas. But just like texts, pictures were *compromises*, *summaries* of reality. The experience he said he had on the scree field, on the other hand, was a sort of 'unabridged' experience of reality. When he found Low his first thought was not 'Oh my God, this person's had a fall. Is there anything I can do to save him?' or anything similar. The strange thing, Aitmatov said, was that he did not immediately regard what he saw as a situation he needed to judge in such or such a way, and certainly not as an *emergency*, even though he realized at once that it was a dead man lying there. Rather, he felt *connected* to the man stretched out on the ground, and had the impression that he had entered an almost infinitely complex pattern. It was as if he were perceiving all the stones, and the colours of the stones, the shimmering and the sound of the raindrops, the features of the dead man's face, the pattern of Low's suit and the shapes which appeared on his shoes when the rain made tracks in the layer of grey dust on the black leather – as if he were perceiving all these in the same detail. All this, he had to repeat to himself, had been *of the present* in a way unfamiliar to him until then, without reference to anything else. He was seized by a feeling of great joy, without knowing why.

He had not yet finished the painting, and he did not know whether the fact that his experience seemed to omit nothing, that it seemed to him as if for a moment he was perceiving the world not *as something*, but as it is, as if he were no longer *perceiving* the world, but as if he actually existed as part of it for the first time, whether this fact made it impossible to paint a picture of the scree field. As children we can find all sorts of shapes in a wet wall or in clouds, which are hauntingly beautiful. Certainly it was not wrong to apply the term 'beauty' to what he had experienced on that occasion. And yet he felt that this word was too banal as a predicate which we always use in our *assessment* of a picture, text or anything else.

Judging by the position of the body at the foot of the rock face, which the painter had photographed with his mobile, Low must have fallen backwards after having scaled about two thirds of the rock face. The Zurich insurance company sent their people to verify this before paying out the death premium. Experts from the mountain rescue service returned to the spot with Aitmatov, where he showed them everything. I myself saw the body laid out at Fluntern Cemetery in Zurich on the day of the funeral. Low did, in fact, have a contented expression on his face, like someone who had finally put something strenuous behind him.

Upset

In the last days before his death, when Low was 'putting the final touches' to the proofs, our conversations had become more dogged. In the three-and-a-half years that we had known each other we had discussed at length philosophy, the academic and non-academic life, politics, science and the arts. It was an inspirational time for both Low and myself. But our last conversation about *Woodcutters* and *Austerlitz*, the novels by Thomas Bernhard and W. G. Sebald, had become tense because I had implied that I felt as if the tone employed by Bernhard in *all* of his works since the prince's speech at the end of the short story 'Gargoyles' had degenerated into a ploy for dealing with every topic in an almost mechanical way. And that although the more gentle Sebald also adopted a constant, unmistakable tone in the modulation of his language, I preferred his writing because in each of his books he addressed the same themes of the unfamiliar, downfall and melancholy, but one never got the impression that he was using a sort of 'linguistic method' to 'batter each topic to death'. I realized at once that my unnecessarily vehement assessment of the authors who we both read and admired had hurt Low. The endlessly taxing discussions about the submissions for the prize must have worn down my intellect, making me commit the error of trying to rank these two masters of language. I still reproach myself today for not seeing, at that moment, that there were two voices present and that it was irrelevant which one was the 'right' one or 'more important' (as if such judgements had any point at all). For I believe that my carelessness damaged my relationship with Low, something I will never be able to make up for now.

For Low – I knew this and it should have stopped me from making the comment – the works of Bernhard had a meaning which transcended the aesthetic. I felt he considered Bernhard's language to be an existential foothold, a substitute for his own voice. My disparaging remark had touched something inviolate, as is often the case with aesthetic (and also political) differences which argument alone cannot eliminate, and thus which are hard to understand for those concerned. The different assumptions which people, on account of their different experiences, start out with when forming judgements cannot 'balance each other out'; we can only accept them and acknowledge that a difference exists. If we fail to accept these differences, but instead try to eliminate or whitewash them, it can only end in conflict. On that occasion I mistakenly tried to gloss over them and so it was inevitable that there would be a cooling in our relationship. After that we exchanged few words, albeit polite ones.

On the Monday in the week when Low died, about a fortnight after our conversation about *Woodcutters* and *Austerlitz*, he called and told me that he would do the last corrections to the second copy of proofs at home and then send them to Munich from his post office in Hanover. That would be the end of his work. He thanked me and hung up with a 'See you again sometime!' I was somewhat saddened by Low's send-off, but did not at the time see it as a warning that he was about to end his life, and nor do I now. It may well have been an accident. Just because someone dies we tend to interpret what they have said and done shortly beforehand as hints of – and preparation for – their demise. In such cases it is the conversations we cannot continue and the misunderstandings we can never rectify that are most difficult to bear, that go through our head time and again and which we interpret as something that must have had a specific relevance to the end of the life we are mourning. I had hoped at some point to be able to clear up the bad feelings that existed between Low and me since our last conversation at the Calenberg Academy, maybe by agreeing that it was absurd to put things in ranking order. The unhappiness I feel at Low's death is mainly due to the fact that we can never put things right between us again.

Low's voice and mine, the voice of Low's daughter and his own remain in an inconclusive relationship. Some aspects of this relationship encouraged further conversation, others stifled it; there were obstacles and moments of elation, too. Such an interplay of voices does not have any goal in its sights, but at the moment when one voice exits, those who remain behind feel as if a goal which has seemingly become an intrinsic part of this interplay can no longer be attained. We often find the exchange of information and opinions tiresome and wish we could avoid it. But the moment someone's death makes it no longer possible, we feel as if we had not said the important things, as if a crucial possibility had been snatched from us to conclude something we had only just begun.

I wonder whether this cooling off in our relationship may have contributed to Low's decision to end his life. Perhaps he thought that essentially there was nothing more to say to me or his daughter, that his world had finally exhausted itself. I know, of course, that we *always* live with unfinished conversations and bad feelings that need to be sorted out, and in most cases these are not followed by suicide, but by continuation, reconciliation and reconnection. Nevertheless I am tortured by the idea that although, thanks to our conversations and his work over the last few years at the Calenberg Academy, Low overcame something akin to a 'remote-controlled' hatred of his academic mentor and a resignation with regard to academic and married life, to return to an active mindset of thinking and friendly discussion, perhaps he felt this new and better state of mind had reached its natural conclusion. He did not *want* to return to the first mindset of hatred and resignation; and perhaps saw no possible future for the other one.

When the publisher heard of Low's death he first asked his widow whether she could find the proofs and see how far work had proceeded on the four prize submissions. Low's widow then called on me, because she felt the task to be beyond her. After going through the proofs I told the publisher that the volume needed no more work. He invited me, now that Low was dead, to write a sort of tribute to him, as well as a concluding piece outlining my opinion on the whole undertaking of the Calenberg Prize, because Low had told the publisher that I had also had a part in choosing the texts.

This is true insofar as I read some of the submissions and discussed them with Low. But right from the beginning I, like Low, was less interested in the arguments presented in the individual essays and in putting them in ranking order, and more concerned with the various *starting points* or *positions* from which, as these papers show, the authors try to answer the question of whether people can be happy. The collection of these starting points seems to me a more interesting aspect of this book than the arguments presented, some more successfully than others, which might induce one to adopt this or that point of view. I am not going to rank these essays, nor will I consider which viewpoint I would be most likely to take myself, for I am not interested in taking positions.

Polyphony and description

Had there still been a jury and had one essay been awarded the *winner's prize* in this competition, this book would never have been published, only the treatise which was the best in the eyes of the commission. When Low said that the liminal situation in which we dealt with these texts – a situation in which there were lots of texts but no prize or jury any more, where there was still an assembly hall in the Academy, but no longer any Academy – that this borderline situation was *ideal*, what he meant was that the intellectual conflicts which always played a part in these competitions, between different jury members as so-called 'representatives' of philosophical 'schools', did not exist in our case. For neither Low nor I saw ourselves as 'representatives' of a philosophical 'position'. Neither of us needed to convince the other, nor anybody else, of the alleged 'superiority' or 'untenability' of certain positions.

Low said he could no longer maintain any position himself, because, in his eyes, the academic world had destroyed him intellectually. I, on the other hand, reject *out of principle* the idea of 'having' or 'representing' a position. Just as Kierkegaard once said his only principle was never to start out with any principle, my position consists of not representing any position to myself or other people, to avoid having to lower myself to the status of someone who stands for a certain viewpoint. For otherwise I would inevitably weaken my ability to view and describe life and the world truthfully. This became clear to me in my conversations with Said Aitmatov, who observed – with his extraordinary mastery of German and with a distance that the non-native speaker has – that 'having' indicates *possession*, whereas he could not regard a conviction or view of the world as a possession which needed to be managed and maintained like a car or an expensive watch. He felt far more that he might *come across* a conviction in conversation or while in thought, or he might *fall into* a particular view of the world, as he did on the Freiberg when he found Low's body in the scree field. Likewise a viewpoint might *vanish* from him or he would *slip out* of a view of the world and by chance find another or slip into it. This, he said, was exactly what happens to a child when they grow up. They do not intentionally change their standpoint by abandoning certain beliefs and accepting others as more plausible. Rather they *grow out* of a certain position towards the world and find themselves *getting into* another, just as he had found Low in the mountains and entered a world view – for a short time at least.

In the conversation when he told me this, Aitmatov and I also agreed that Nietzsche had expressed it very accurately in paragraph fifty-five of *The Anti-Christ*, when he described the person with a tendency towards convictions as an enemy of the truth. Here Nietzsche wonders, very generally, 'whether convictions are not more dangerous enemies of the truth than lies . . .' He goes on: 'What I mean by lies is *not* wanting to see something that you see, not wanting to see something as you see it . . . The most common lie is the one you deceive yourself with . . . This *not* wanting to see what you see, this not wanting to see something as you see it is almost the first requirement for those who take sides . . . The person who takes sides inevitably becomes a liar.' Aitmatov and I also agreed with Nietzsche that there are questions 'about which man cannot decide the truth and falsehood. All of the highest questions, all the highest problems of valuation are beyond human reason . . . True philosophy is recognizing the limits of human reason.'

Aitmatov added that this was also true of painting: he could only paint a picture which he felt corresponded to the truth when he was at the limit of his ability to judge. Every judgement about a face or a landscape ruined the possibility of reproducing what he had seen. If he made a judgement about a face, be it villainous or saintly, he was no longer capable of painting what his eye saw. If he made a judgement about a landscape, be it spoiled by development or 'untouched', he would *illustrate* this judgement and the emotions accompanying it in his picture, but he would not paint the truth of the landscape.

By contrast, Low believed himself to be a *failure* in his positionlessness. He rejected Nietzsche as a relativist; he said his philosophy was full of contradictions. Low believed that anybody who did not see the world from a particular standpoint basically did not see it at all. He had lost the capacity to develop his own position by constantly having to take and check other standpoints at university. Low thought he would never be able to make up this supposed loss, and it is what had turned him into a melancholic person. My insistence that he had not lost anything in this respect fell on deaf ears. Unlike Low I am deliberately and I must say I think *successfully positionless*, and my positionlessness is a constant source of happiness. For I do not wish to view the world from a specific standpoint, but want to exist in it. I would be deliberately weakening my consciousness of belonging to the world if I perched myself on an opinion from which to survey it. It was a common positionlessness but with different moods which brought Low and me together. We shared something fundamental, but our states of mind were alien to each other, and this is why we were so interested in the other. It is what fed our conversations and I had the impression that my role in our friendship was to prevent his melancholy from descending into despair.

After my discussion with Said Aitmatov I thought that the satisfied or even cheerful expression on Low's dead face may have been a result of his having lost his footing. Maybe at the moment of death when hitting the scree field – as with any fall from such a height the person dies immediately from the shock of impact – he had for the first time become aware of the exhilaration of falling. Maybe at that moment he was able for the first time to enjoy the sensation of having no foothold and no longer needing to search for one.

Low and I were agreed that the idea that philosophy or science were all about 'representing' this or that set of propositions could be traced back to a very specific and limited view of the history of thought. If we look at the 'original contrast' in the philosophy of antiquity between Plato and Aristotle, we see that even here it is not a contrast between two 'representatives' of different sets of propositions, but between a philosophy which *does not* stand for anything specific (Plato's) and a differentiated *representative philosophy* (Aristotle's).

In fact, in the entire history of thought Aristotle is the most successful and influential representative of a philosophy which makes *assertions* and *represents* these assertions with justifications, or argues their case. Plato, on the other hand, *presents* a variety of possible positions in his various dialogues. He does this in a different way from Aristotle in the proems of his discourses. There Aristotle merely summarizes the standpoints that have (apparently) been previously taken, in order to distance his own position from them. Even though Socrates plays a privileged role in the Platonic dialogues, individuals such as Protagoras, Parmenides and Timaeus figure no less impressively and independently in Plato's writings. Plato's philosophy, as we know it from his dialogues, is *many-voiced*, *polyphonic*. It discusses the different possibilities of thought and relations to one another. Even Socrates does not always assert this or that, but often highlights in the maieutic processes of his conversational techniques the standpoints of his interlocutors, focusing on showing what connects them, what follows from them. This sort of polyphonic philosophy is a process of *making people aware* of viewpoints, *articulating* them, a *display* of different voices.

The question of what *unwritten theories* Plato himself advocated besides the dialogues ruins the contrast between a monophonic philosophy that *asserts* and a polyphonic one that *shows*. Even if Plato may have championed verbally a theory he never wrote down, as his seventh letter seems to suggest, this does not necessarily mean that philosophy must always boil down to a conclusion, a theory in which this or that is declared and verified to be the ultimate truth. In Plato's writings and later, too, philosophy has *repeatedly* been polyphonic. If we regard the Wittgenstein of the *Tractatus* and that of the *Philosophical Investigations* as two voices and observe Wittgenstein's wish that both works be published in the same volume, Wittgenstein is a polyphonic philosopher. The same is true of Schelling in his different phases and projects: we have the voices of transcendental, natural, identity and later positive philosophy. And how else should we describe Hegel's *Phenomenology of Spirit* if not as a polyphonic philosophy? It has been noted that this work by Hegel continues aspects of the Platonic dialogues; that Hegelian dialectics and Platonic dialogics belong together as different ways of presenting a variety of philosophical positions in conflict, which in Hegel gives rise to a process of development. Kierkegaard's book *Either/Or* is also polyphonic, in the sense that it presents a philosophical–existential alternative, while it is hard to say how many voices ultimately speak through Nietzsche, the 'mask-wearer'. Finally, in Ernst Cassirer's *Philosophy of Symbolic Forms*, the writings of Mikhail Bakhtin and Nelson Goodman's *Ways of Worldmaking*, many-voiced, non-assertive philosophy acquires a methodological awareness in the twentieth century.

Sometimes many voices may be heard in one head over a short period of time. Sometimes the different voices characterize *phases* in the chapters of a thinking person's life, as with Schelling or Wittgenstein. Who knows whether Spinoza – had he not died shortly after finishing his *Ethics* – might not have developed another voice like Wittgenstein, who wanted to bury himself alive in his life as a teacher after his *Tractatus*; whether Spinoza might not have written something analogous to the *Philosophical Investigations* after his *Ethics*? Voices need time to develop, then they appear in reaction to what has already been said, including by oneself. Dying early is thus the best way, apart from stubbornness, of remaining monophonic.

Polyphony has always been widespread in literature. The most famous example is the novelistic art of Fyodor Dostoevsky, highlighted by the Soviet theoretician Mikhail Bakhtin. Unlike in his theoretical writings, where Dostoevsky appears strangely at sea, in his novels he devotes all his intellectual energy to producing a multitude of voices. In a sense, Dostoevsky himself saw the characters he produced with language as autonomous. Bakhtin then developed a whole theory of polyphony, which sadly has only really received the attention it deserves in literary theory, less in philosophy. But even though philosophers generally *reject* their voices from the past and claim that they 'were wrong' back then and had to correct themselves, this *development* by thinkers is often a changing of the basic premises from which they philosophize. Not all readers change with them. Often they find the earlier positions more plausible than the later ones, as is the case with the Heidelberg philosopher Erhard Scheibe, who always regarded the early Wittgenstein as plausible, but the later one peculiar and wayward. Similarly, there are many more philosophers who focus on Schelling's early voices than on his positive and rather Catholic later philosophy.

Clearly, readers do not see a process of maturity towards the truth when a philosopher changes premises.

Almost everybody thinks that if a change occurs in their thinking, the later position must be the one which is closest to the truth, and the earlier position a fallacy, only because it deviates from the later one. But this might be a fallacy in itself. Maybe the choice of premise cannot be justified philosophically. If a person starts from a variety of premises *at the same time* and allows a variety of voices to speak *at the same time*, they are bound to get into difficulty. Hearing voices is, after all, a psychopathological symptom when it does not occur in a novelist while writing fiction. But a diachronic succession of voices in a person's lifetime may be nothing more than the natural consequence of the changes in the basis of experience for the process of thinking over the course of a life. In particular, the experience of the actual consequences of taking a certain position during one's life may in many cases lead to the appearance of new premises for thought. It is true that there are some people who cannot experience in this way, not even with their own thoughts. I am not talking about such people here, however, but about philosophical minds. Only these draw the intellectual consequences from their life and monitor the consequences their philosophy has for their life; or they are forced to note with horror (in contrast to the academic philistines) that their philosophizing has absolutely no consequences for their life at all.

If there are as many premises for thought as there are starting points for experience, then we need only imagine other possible starting points for our own experience to arrive at other premises for thought. It is very easy to imagine how differently our life may have gone if we had not experienced this or had we really experienced that. In every person there is a variety of possible starting points for experiences. For example, how would we gauge our current life situation if we had fought in a war, or if we had *not* experienced a war we should have fought in? Do not all people who are old have to ask such questions when in conversation with their children, and likewise all children with their parents in order to understand the thinking of the other? Do not all of us, at some point in our lives, wonder how we would have judged Person A *today* if we had met Person B *before* rather than *after* them? Perhaps, like Robert Musil, we need a certain appreciation of possibility in order to be able to perceive these possible starting points succinctly in ourselves. Maybe writers only really act out in their characters the possibilities of experience and life which are in their own existences. It is obvious, however, that those people whose appreciation of possibility is weak and who never explore the fictional possibilities of their own experiences, lives and thinking, overrate the premises they are endowed with as *necessary*. From our own inner perspective (not differentiated by fictional exercises) our character and the course of its development is always necessary; 'from outside', however, it appears random. People who cannot conceive that other people start from other premises thus appear unimaginative.

The presentation or demonstration and description of states of mind and starting points can be valuable in itself because it can lead to discoveries if it occurs with the necessary precision. We tend to think that knowledge is only advanced by explanations and conclusions. But the thing being described does not have the same precision and incisiveness *prior to* the description, as it appears to have *in* and *after* a good description. A good description *extracts* features and structures from the thing being described, thereby making something visible in the same way that a microscope or telescope makes something visible. The juxtaposition of descriptions gives rise to contrasts which highlight aspects of the thing being described more clearly than without the contrast. This is known from Goethe and the late Wittgenstein as the 'perspicuous overview' method. Such an overview provides us with a *succinctness of experience* which, unlike *explanation*, does not attribute one thing to another, thereby continually simplifying the complexities of reality.

Said Aitmatov once told me that although he can see something that makes an impression on him, it is not until he paints it that he is conscious of *what* he is seeing. Then he sees *more and more* and finally understands why a particular view attracted him. For him painting is a means of eliminating the formulas and judgements that put themselves between him and the world, making his own intuition unintelligible. He starts painting and then sees on the canvas that what he has painted is not what he has seen. Painting thus becomes for him a self-critique of his sense of sight. It is only when painting that he asks himself what he has *really* seen. It has nothing to do with photographic accuracy. After all, even a photograph only very seldom – when taken by an artist – reproduces what we see in a way that it is only when we look at the photograph that we realize what we have seen. A striking view produces something inside us, and what it produces inside us has, in turn, an effect on what we see. The painting must document this interplay, Aitmatov said. The truth of what we see when we really see something individual is not a truth that can be registered in general assessments. It is the truth, Aitmatov insisted, of an endless complexity of forms, colours, feelings and thoughts. As a manifestation of this endless complexity a picture must compromise as little as possible; only in this way can the truth appear when viewing the picture, too. The philosophical teaching that truth is mainly concerned with judgements and propositions is false, he said, because the endeavour to be honest towards one's own complexity and that of the world has nothing to do with the process of forming judgements, which is always one of condemnation. Just as a judge cannot help but reduce the person to the crime they have committed, and the truth about a person in a criminal trial boils down to finding out whether the accused has committed the crime or not, the judgement of perception which says that this is hot or cold, beautiful or ugly, light or dark, simplifies what is seen into these yes–no contrasts. One might almost say, therefore, that the person who passes judgement is lying, because they are denying the complexities which exist beyond these simple contrasts in the judgement.

If philosophy could align itself more closely with painting as Aitmatov conceives it, and made an effort to reveal the variety of starting points for thought and the complex contents of our experience, it would, in my view, be taking an important development. For acknowledging the individual differences in life, experience and thought has quite rightly been seen as a prerequisite of human happiness. Anybody who fails to acknowledge these differences or get them clear in their mind either feels alienated by the otherness, or suffers from the lie of trying to make themselves and others appear as 'basically' the same to escape the experience of alienation. If, even under these conditions, it is still clear that we are not the same and think on the basis of different premises, either this needs to be *combated* as an error or *suppressed* as a false impression. Both of these make us unhappy. Everything which ends in a hopeless battle against the complexity of reality – be it our own complexity or the inexhaustibility of 'the world' – prevents happiness.

At the beginning of this book Low talks about his life and mentions that something unknown happened to him in adolescence, which prevented him from being happy for the rest of his life. It estranged him from his parents and he built up an anger towards them. This goes back to the fact that he was unable to recognize the differences and unfamiliarity between himself and other people, because he lacked the necessary courage and strength, or because there was nobody to help him develop this courage and strength. When we realize that we are different from our parents, that we do not agree with them, this experience of unfamiliarity with people who were the closest to us up until that point leads readily to a rejection, either of ourselves or our parents, or both. This inevitably goes hand in hand with a painful feeling of a loss of security. We are no longer at home in the world and cannot find a home in it any more unless we manage to exist ourselves as almost independent amongst the different, almost independent existences in the world. For this we need to learn to recognize that the endlessly complex differences which make up the world are intrinsic to independence. The loss of childhood security, however, is often followed by a forlorn search – one which affects our entire existence – for people or environments that we imagine are *not* alien to us. Most people's lives are not determined by the possibility of their own (if limited) independence and taking pleasure in this, but by suffering from *separateness*.

I believe that Low undertook this search his whole life in the effort to find a philosophical friendship which corresponded with his ideal of the Bloomsbury Group. He was never successful and so suffered throughout his life. For in his search he would switch between spurning others who remained strangers to him and rejecting his own self, because he was not able to make a 'connection' with other people. The fact that his time at the Academy made him unhappy was probably a result of this high expectation of philosophical friendship and mistakenly seeking this friendship at the university.

Low's fundamental error, if we can speak of such a thing, was to have switched with a sense of expectation from veterinary medicine to philosophy after the party with his student neighbours. For in the university world, where there is a strong pressure to conform, the likelihood of finding one's own voice, and tolerating and appreciating the otherness of one's peers is very low. Even on just an *intellectual*, rather than existential level, he seems to have acknowledged the variety of voices, including his own, in his work on the texts for the Calenberg Prize, although we might question whether this selection really does present standpoints that are particularly 'far apart'.

What was Low looking for when he trying to make friendships such as allegedly existed within the Bloomsbury Group or as he thought he had found at Leonard's party? Perhaps the specific type of debate which the American philosopher Stanley Cavell once outlined in conversation. Asked why he had studied clarinet and not piano, like his mother, Cavell answered that he had never wanted to learn a solo instrument, but always wanted to play in a band, a jazz band. In response to Adorno's rejection of jazz as a sort of musical competition, Cavell said, 'Oh Adorno never really understood jazz. When the members of a band take turns to play variations on the theme, it's not about finding a winner. It's about the theme, what you can make of it. Everyone's delighted when someone manages to play a completely unexpected and brand-new variation. The band members try to boost each other and the theme. Shouldn't conversation be like that, too?'

There are many types of friendship: those which help business, those which satisfy desire, and those which advance power. There are cold communities of competition, where conflict produces a winner; and there are warm communities of value, where people mutually assert their shared beliefs and defend them 'to the outside world'. Low found all of this without looking for it. He was probably seeking what Cavell was talking about: an exchange of ideas and counter-ideas that was neither competitive nor wholly consensual from the outset; one which deepened or intensified the meaning of what was being discussed, not aimed at finding a victor or agreement, but at a new insight which showed the topic of discussion in a different light from before.

Low was disappointed that knowledge in the Academy was produced only for the advancement of people, but that there were no longer any communities of people who existed only for the advancement of knowledge, even though the life of individuals in a community which focused not on their own advancement but that of knowledge would probably be the happiest, i.e., the one most conducive to the advancement of the individuals. Luck is like knowledge, friendship and love: you cannot force it, want and *produce* it directly; the desire to produce happiness can only prevent it. Nonetheless you need to tend to it and make an effort so that it appears. Most human communities are unhappy because they are characterized by this desire to make things happen: victory, pleasure, power, solidarity, knowledge – we are supposed to *pursue* these with every ounce of our will and *make* them technically correct. Nowadays we also tend to *assess* whether we are on the right track. This approach systematically puts flight to what we are striving for. For nobody is surprised by knowledge, love or pleasure which is *made* or *produced*, which means it can never live up to expectations. This is not necessarily due to a lack of intensity, but because it cannot stand for itself; it is compared to what was expected. The crudeness of comparison does not permit independence or makes it unrecognizable. Anybody who has a *benchmark* is lost, downtrodden by the comparison. The unexpected can only occur when something appears 'by itself'; something not wanted or planned because it could not be imagined in the first place. What is required for the unimaginable to appear is the dedicated interaction of very different forces, not directly in opposition, but conscious of the variety of the actors, just as the clarinet, piano, double bass and drums do not play against each other in the band, but conscious of the variety of these instruments. They all have their own voice and yet can play variations on the same theme.

For Low this collection of essays represented an acknowledgement of differences and the possibility of analysing them. For such a project it is unfortunate that contemporary philosophical efforts are geared to aping the individual sciences and, like these, producing unifying explanations and universal theories to substantiate these explanations. (What exacerbates it is the capitalist spirit of having to compare everything in a market which has since gripped the sciences and philosophy, too, and no longer allows independent thinking which does not *wish* to afford comparison.) I hesitated before going ahead with Low's plan to publish these texts, as it seemed that the essays do not fit into the contemporary landscape of philosophy and literature.

If you wanted to put something aside from current developments in philosophy which might have a chance of being noticed, it would not necessarily just be essays like this. More important would be to undertake the theoretical work for a *descriptive philosophy of differences* which does not lose itself in the murky waters of a 'thinking of difference', something that already existed in the twentieth century. One would have to explain the differences between, on the one hand, the philosophical description of many starting points for experiences and thought, and of the many voices that emerge from these; and on the other, a positionlessness which finds no voice. Such an explanation would have to answer a great many questions. For example, what does description mean, and how would such a *descriptive* philosophy relate to a *critical* one? To what extent is a description of something an attempt to remove the need for comparison and recognize it in its uniqueness? What relevance do such descriptive truths about differences have for life in contrast to unifying theories? Would it be possible with a description of differences to put a stop to the unhappiness of unifying theory and comparison? Or would this just represent another overestimation of philosophy? But I gave up long ago thinking it was my job to answer such questions to explain Low's selection. For I am finished with those sorts of academic investigations.

Gabriel Kolk
Pattensen
July

Afterword

Karim Bschir strongly advised me not to write this Afterword. I understand and share his reservations about people trying to explain themselves. But there were requests for explanations of what has just gone. So I decided to provide some.

Regarding happiness as the ultimate goal of our actions is a widespread interpretation of human life. But this goal does not *necessarily* have to be bound up with life; it could, as Raymond Geuss has shown in his essay 'Happiness and Politics' have *developed* historically. Just like death, the pursuit of happiness seems to be a sort of 'anthropological constant'. But the fact that something akin to the experience of happiness exists in every culture, and that all of us die, does not mean that happiness and death do not have a history. The quest for fame and status, as it might have influenced life in Homeric times, and still influences it today on the sports field (or in the army) and in show business (or in politics), is perhaps an *alternative* to the pursuit of happiness and need not – as I did in the text with the voice of Lalitha Dakini (or Spinoza) – be interpreted as a *failed pursuit of happiness*. In the past there may have been people – and still a few individuals today, too – who *consciously sacrificed* happiness for fame and status. Today, however, many believe that fame makes you happy and a life devoted to attaining fame and status is also one where happiness is pursued. (Perhaps we could say something similar about striving for pleasure.) Only historical and empirical social research can establish how these things actually relate to each other. The intent of this book was to produce neither these histories nor a 'theory' of the supposed constants of happiness and death. But the historical Aristotelian or Buddhist *view* that *all* people strive to find happiness was one of the two *chief focuses* of these experimental reflections. I asked myself what this view was actually about and what we can recognize in it if we treat it experimentally, each time slightly varying the standpoint.

Death or how we deal with our own mortality was the second topic of these investigations. It is linked to the first, the pursuit of happiness. For in the view outlined above, our dealings with our own mortality seem to be a *motif* and *principle* in the shaping of human existence. Religions and cultural projects which span generations, such as the sciences which are committed to progress, primarily focus on interpreting the finitude of human life and overcoming the difficulties which the knowledge of death entails. If we apply the quantitative measure of life length, *every* life can be viewed as imperfect, because it could have lasted a little longer. Only a few people might see *immortality* as a requirement of happiness; indeed, one could take the opposing view and argue that an infinite life would *devalue* human existence. But the finitude of human life was not only a cause for regret in European antiquity, where they distinguished between the happy immortals with 'no destiny' and the 'suffering' mortals. In the modern era, too, finitude has been described as a blemish of existence, an inherent imperfection or as a 'metaphysical evil'.

The *method* with which the two topics of happiness and death are dealt with here is no longer a common one in established contemporary academic literature on philosophy. It might be helpful, therefore, to say a few words about it. I *experimented* with different interpretations of happiness and different meanings of death in the four essays, which were all based on different premises, comparable to the different positions of the characters on the God hypothesis in Hume's *Dialogues Concerning Natural Religion* (Chapters 2 to 4). A *fictional narrative framework* described the relevance of these topics and reflected narratively the relations between the theoretical positions in two possible lives: Low and Kolk (chapters 1 and 6). I was guided by the belief that *discovering* and *showing* various philosophical standpoints, in contrast to a phenomenology with an analytical academic agenda, is an independent and justifiable alternative to explanatory undertakings in philosophy. Such a descriptive philosophy must, however, operate closer to the literary sphere than does phenomenology. It was this belief which gave rise to the structure of my book. With topics such as 'happiness' and 'death' I regard the understanding of different starting points or voices in contrasting accounts – a *description of polyphony* from which the text gets its generic label 'philosophical compendium'– as an *end in itself*. In this respect the book's structure is closely linked to one of the viewpoints it aims to highlight, and which is particularly important to me: Cavell's view that *acknowledging difference* is the key to happiness and that an inability to accept difference is the first step to unhappiness. To be able to recognize, observe and tolerate differences – not all! – relating to matters that are absolutely 'elementary' to human life is a form of *serenity*. The constant need to remove, eliminate or unify these differences, on the other hand, can lead to various forms of pointless aggression. In this sense, the relentless pursuit of understanding and consensus on very fundamental issues denotes an inability to remain serene.

The difference between the view of one person who sees 5 as the sum of 3 and 4, and another who sees it as the result of adding 3 and 2, is certainly *not* one that could be described as polyphony. On the other hand, the differences between the basic convictions of a religious person, such as Lalitha Dakini, and a non-religious one, such as Erwin Weinberger, cannot be placed on a single scale of 'true' and 'false'. In this case we have different *voices* or *registers* of human existence *within* which certain utterances are true and others false. Here it makes as little sense to say that Weinberger is right and Dakini mistaken as it does to maintain that tigers are true animals, but snails false ones, even though we can differentiate ill tigers from healthy ones and ill snails from healthy ones.

Identifying *when* we are dealing with the difference between true and false within a *single* voice or a single register of existence and when we encounter a *change* in voice or register is often a difficult philosophical question in itself. But when working with the topics of 'death' and 'happiness' in this book, I felt it was relatively simple to answer. As Erwin Weinberger correctly notes, some postmodern thinkers are too casual in their dealings with polyphony and believe, for example, that even the answers to the questions of whether the sun is a fixed star or not or whether a cholera pathogen existed before it was discovered in 1884 by Robert Koch depend on one's 'standpoint'. This is surely not true.

The description of many voices, as presented by a dialogue or this imagined 'philosophical compendium', is an *acknowledgement* of difference. By contrast, a philosophy of disambiguation, which *always* attempts to *decide* between *fundamental* standpoints or different registers of life, is a way of thinking that ultimately refuses to accept fundamental differences. At the very least it can be a theoretical step on the path to unhappiness. My *content-focused* approach to happiness made it necessary from the start to deal with the subject in a form which presented multiple voices or differences, such as a dialogue, correspondence or the 'philosophical compendium' chosen here.

Voices can determine the course of someone's life as well as forms of thinking and research in the sciences. Weinberger is a voice that represents the *explanatory sciences* such as physics or biology; Dakini a voice that represents a religious *view on life*. Because life and science mutually influence one another, we need to juxtapose voices of religiously motivated life forms with voices from the sciences. When faced with the fundamental alternatives in life or when choosing between 'registers' of existence we cannot, however, rewind and make the decision again, according to scientific or religious principles, of whether we will let our lives be determined by the sciences or religion, or by leading a 'test life' in one of the registers. Nor is there a 'meta-life' beyond the scientifically or religiously oriented existence, in which we could find principles to direct us in existential choices of this sort. As Paul Feyerabend says, we decide to be with a particular partner, take a particular career and live in a particular country, *without a pre-existing knowledge* of all the possibilities and impossibilities these choices entail. Instead, the possibilities and impossibilities arise and appear in the life we have chosen. It is an illusion spread by life and happiness coaches that we can use a 'checklist' to work out in advance how to shape our lives and what principles we should base our decisions on, thereby sparing us the life experience. After a certain period of time, moreover, it is no longer possible to return to square one with decision-making, because we have changed ourselves and the world with the process of life experience and actions based on our decisions.

Feyerabend says that something similar is true of science. Science, too, decides to pursue particular topics with particular methods without the assistance of any pre-existing, irrefutable meta-principles allowing it to choose *scientifically* between all possible topics and methods. These are a dream of evaluators of scientific projects and universalist epistemologists. If Feyerabend is right, however, a theory of all science that believes it can provide such principles in advance of all scientific experience is just as misguided as the life and happiness coaches who work on the cookbook model. In their basic aspects, life and the sciences both develop *historically* (and not planned) as they proceed. Life and scientific work do not begin only after their forms have been sensibly organized according to higher principles and tested in advance. If, in this development, fundamentally different forms have appeared which live and think, all the observer can do is *describe critically* the polyphony, giving rise to a number of questions. What is possible in this way of life or form of thinking? What is the price for this being possible? What is ruled out now and what is always impossible? What can be changed and what not?

Clearly, Kolk's voice is prominent in this compendium. But it is not a voice which speaks from another theoretical position in parallel to the 'standpoints' of the fictional prize authors, i.e., it is not on the same level as the voices in the four essays, nor does it represent a position from which the essays could be *judged*. Kolk's position is precisely one which *refuses* to adopt a 'right' theoretical stance towards the world, but tries to *exist as part of* the world, discovering what has a certain level of independence in the world (stones, plants, people, philosophies) and recognizing this autonomy. Kolk's piece was conceived as the result of a very different activity from all the other writings in this book (including Low's writings about himself). Kolk's writing comes from a position which is *practical* on the one hand, but can also be characterized as *philosophical*. It leads to an activity which undertakes the *observation* and *description* of all standpoints for its own sake, but *avoids* adopting a *particular* one. One could call this position one of *allegiance* to the many individuals in the world without denying one's own individuality, i.e., without *identifying* with an individuality other than one's own, which would mean a loss of one's own voice.

Kolk's comments should also be seen as an acknowledgement of difference; they result from a deep immersion in these differences. The writing and reading of the ideas articulated by the four voices here should be viewed as a form of intellectual *exercise*, as an *exercitium* or *meditatio*. For voices or registers of existence are also things which exist as part of the world and in which we can immerse ourselves. Above all, however, we recognize the roles that *theories* of happiness do not play, only because we 'pass through' these theories and recognize their ineffectiveness as explanatory undertakings in life. This process is a practical precondition for the view that the business of asserting and explaining is meaningless in the search for the perfect life.

Reading this book should thus be seen as therapy for theorizing about happiness.

To illustrate the significance of a position of self-forgetting or immersion, and the related activity which produces a descriptive representation rather than any explanatory theory, we could also modify a phrase of Wittgenstein's: 'We realize the solution to the problem of life when this problem vanishes. (Is this not the reason why people who, after much doubt, become aware of the meaning of life but cannot say what this meaning of life is?)' If we substitute 'happiness' for 'meaning' and 'life' here, the phrase runs like this: 'We realize the solution to the problem of happiness when this problem vanishes. (Is this not the reason why people who have found a happy life cannot say what this happiness consists of?)' It is only if you believe you have to attain a particular theoretical knowledge to be happy (or discover a meaning to life) that you might think you could assert what happiness (or the meaning of life) consists of. Kolk cannot say which belief *about* the world or people makes us happy, because he does not believe that *any* conviction which is simply *about* something can make us happy, or that to have it is a requirement of happiness. Rather Kolk believes that happiness lies only in the ability to exist as part of the world, alongside other beings unfamiliar to us, so that one does not merely view the world from the outside or explain away and 'devalue' the otherness in it, by distancing oneself with ratings and playing judge with regard to its individuals.

Although Kolk's non-theorizing voice predominates here, Kolk is not me. For I lack the ability to differentiate between minerals or look after a garden (and exist as part of the world in this way), nor do I possess the fortune which allows Kolk

– unlike Low, who is financially and existentially dependent on the Academy – to preserve his intellectual autonomy. For this reason – unlike Kolk – I am also intrigued by the question of *how* a faithful description of differences can produce the intended insight. But a theory about knowledge gained from the demonstration of difference could only come about from future research into knowledge gleaned from faithful description. Key here would be an investigation into how description can give rise to meaning and steer our attention.

Some of the ideas in these texts stem from sketches I began but never finished in the mid-1980s for a fictional dialogue between prisoners in Nazi Germany about death and happiness before their executions. The material I collected for this was used in a seminar on death, which I gave at Kassel University in 1998, and for lectures on happiness, practice and technology I have been giving at the Swiss Federal Institute of Technology in Zurich. After opting for an imagined 'philosophical compendium' instead of a dialogue to represent polyphony within this topic, I had *real*, non-fictional conversations with Bruno Contestabile in Zurich on utility, happiness and risk, which stimulated some of the content. In my venture to come up with the actual literary form for this book, which at first existed only in my imagination, my ideas on philosophical methodology have been influenced, and my knowledge of this reinforced through discussions with, and reading texts by, Peter Bieri, Stanley Cavell, Wolfram Eilenberger, Raymond Geuss, Sibylla Lotter and Lutz Wingert, although some of them did not know what I was working on. Even if their writings and the conversations I have had with them since 2006 on the significance of descriptions and explanations, argumentation and fiction, and genealogical and 'time-transcending' reflections in philosophy did not directly address the topics of happiness and death, they were nevertheless of great benefit to my work on this book. For all the above-named people demonstrate in their own works that timidity is the only reason for sticking with the standardized forms of philosophical writing – which are not only ubiquitous, but regrettably deemed obligatory almost everywhere – if you consider them unsuitable for expressing your own way of thinking. I give my thanks to all these people, as well as to the students who have taken part in my seminars and lectures on the topics addressed in this book for the suggestions they have given me verbally and in writing.

Peter Bieri, Karim Bschir, David Gugerli, Tobias Heyl and Gisela Neukomm read through the manuscript before it reached the print stage, offering sympathetic comments and improving the text in places. I would like to thank them, too, for their honest and friendly judgements and suggestions for shortening what was originally a longer book.

Combining fiction with theoretical reflection, as I have done in this volume, is a long-established form in the tradition of philosophical writing. The linking and mutual reflection of theoretical reasoning and narrative can be found in philosophical works from Plato via Thomas More, Montaigne and Voltaire to Kierkegaard and Camus (and currently in the writing of Pascal Mercier aka Peter Bieri). It may appear arrogant to try to place oneself in this tradition. But the fact that there have always been books like this makes me confident that there will also continue to be readers for these sorts of works. However, although this book is dedicated to my son, I cannot be certain in my hope that he will be amongst its readers someday. But when we do something together I stop thinking about myself and the world with my professional hat on and start being part of the world. For this reason his contribution to the book is not inconsiderable.

Michael Hampe
Zurich
January 2009

Notes

Chapter One

p. 28 'Before Newton… as possessing a soul': cf Gilbert, 1958, p. 308.
p. 28 'Goethe still believed light to be divine': cf Schöne, 1987.
p. 28 'around 1900 Hans Driesch… procreation': Driesch, 1909.
p. 29 'Likewise Galileo's telescope… divine world': cf Toulmin and Goodfield, 1961.
p. 30 'If progress… beliefs belong, too': This is the so-called 'pessimistic induction' from the history of science, cf Laudan, 1981.
p. 30 'In fact, however, we are moving… is progress': cf Niiniluoto, 1979 and 2007.
p. 31 'Today we know… scientific development', cf Miller, 1974; Psillos, 1999; Tichy, 1974.
p. 31 'As long as we understand… are incommensurable': cf Kuhn, 1962; Feyerabend, 1975.
p. 31 'But even if I do not know… 6,000 years': Newton, 1950; Westfall, 1980.
p. 33 'These languages are… old terminology': cf Hagner and Rheinberger, 1998; Rheinberger, 2000; Hampe, 2007, pp. 154–64.
p. 33 'We need only consider… are concerned': cf Wolkenhauer, 2001.
p. 34 'Back in 1853… algebra': Grassmann, 1853.
p. 34 'as Plato says in the *Timaeus*': Plato, *Timaeus*, 29c.
p. 36 'According to Vico… created themselves': cf Vico, 1730/2000 and Morrison, 1978.
p. 36 'But the printed circuit board… problems': cf Pircher, 2005.
p. 36f 'The linking of… is nonsense': cf von Foerster, 1985.
p. 38 'Our examples show… human brain': cf Gehlen, 1957.
p. 41 'In order to pacify… they give rise to': cf Freud, 1948.
p. 41 'Civilisation offers us… dying people': cf Elias, 1982.
p. 41 'As we have known… belong together': Rousseau, 1914.
p. 42 'Religions are particularly dangerous… live out their lives': cf Kakar, 1997.
p. 45 'Stephen Toulmin… from his enemy': cf Toulmin, 1972, pp. 52–84.
p. 46 'This flexibilzation… improve their situation': cf Sennett, 1998.
p. 47 'This is why it is necessary… the suffering': cf Elias, 1983, pp. 7–72.
p. 47 '"Some people think it reasonable… value judgements"': Jankélévitch, 2007, p. 87.
p. 49 'The postmodern rejection… global capitalism': from a conversation with Lutz Wingert.
p. 50 'In the last century… non-formal languages': Tarski 1949 and 1969.
p. 50 'Anybody who doubts… Bernard Williams has shown': Williams, 2002, Ch. 9.
p. 51f 'If, on the other hand… a *miracle*': cf Boyd, 1973.

p. 55f 'Set against these... gravitational force': cf Weinberg, 2001, p. 199.
p. 56 'The longer modern science... subjected to experiment': cf Dewey, 1938/2002, p. 533f.
p. 57 'The result of this... intensification of experience': cf Whitehead, 1929/1978, p. 109.
p. 58 '"People were bored... simplest passport photos"': Köhlmeier, 2007, p. 97.
p. 62 'If I have a tumour... would have us believe': cf Weizsäcker, 2005.
p. 66 'From a *functional* perspective... appears to be imminent': cf Spinoza, *Ethica* IV, Proposition 67.
p. 66 'This sort of thinking... evolutionary pressure': cf Tugendhat, 2007, p. 165.
p. 67 '"find it hard to imagine... criminality"': Jankélévitch, 2007, p. 13.
p. 67 '"absolute tragedy"... "secret"': Jankélévitch, 2007, p. 14f.
p. 68 '"We are attracted by... power of attraction"': Nuland, 1993, p. 15.
p. 69 '"The oval opening... window panes"': Nádas, 2002, pp. 279, 281.
p. 71 'If we see our life... this stream of experience': cf Parfit, 1984, p. 281f.
p. 72f 'An epistemological argument... than the former': cf Hume, 1975, p. 113 and Hampe, 1997, p. 73f.
p. 74f 'It is often claimed... *Galilean* methods': cf Lewin, 1981.
p. 75 '"*Individuum est ineffabile*"... outlined above': cf Hampe, 1996, p. 53 and the literature referred to there.
p. 75 'Building on... Lewin writes': Cassirer, 1910.
p. 75 '"It is not the tendency... quantification"': Lewin, 1981, p. 242.
p. 79 'A consensual approach... conceptual differences': Groeben, 1992.
p. 79 'There has to be agreement... Galilean method': cf Ros, 1990, p. 8.
p. 80 'The idea of such apparatuses is not new': I have Michael Hagner to thank for this piece of information.
p. 80 'As far back as 1928... "brain mirror"': Carnap, 1928/1979, § 167.
p. 80 'And even before Carnap... "pictures of the soul"': cf Hagner, 2006, pp. 228, 232.
p. 85 'This difference has... "meaning"': Schmid, 2007.
p. 86 'It has been argued... "subjects"': Rohs, 1996, p. 12 (following Bröcker, 1977, p. 25).

Chapter Three

p. 91 'as Stanley Cavell puts it in response to Ludwig Wittgenstein': Cavell, 2005, p. 112.
p. 93 'as Spinoza... *Intellectus Emendatione*': Spinoza, 1925, Vol. II, p. 5f.
p. 94 'Traditionally this process... education': Meister Eckehart, 1963, p. 352f.
p. 97 '"action"... "alienation"... "the relationship itself... above man"': Marx, 1966, p. 248.
p. 97f 'The human need... realize their life's plans': cf Sennett, 1998.
p. 98 'However, the basic realization... Aristotle, for example': Aristotle, 1979, 1122a.
p. 99 'If, as Aristotle did... drinking water': Aristotle, 1971, p. 1330b.
p. 101 'The pursuit of power... "solitary, poor, nasty, brutish and short"': Hobbes, 1991, p. 89.

p. 103 'Once someone has… elaborated this idea, too': Hobbes, 1991, p. 88.
p. 103 'We can say that ambition… space as possible,' Jankélévitch, 2007, p. 127.
p. 106 'All this was already known… Houllebecq, for example': Epictetus, 1984, p. 22 and Houllebecq, 1994.
p. 107 'At the end of Beckett's… neither of them moves': Beckett, 1960, p. 116.
p. 109 '"*suffering*" is not a scientific concept': Michaelis, 1958: XXXIII.
p. 109 'Although biology… problem-solving': Popper, 1994.
p. 109 '"There is… a total contradiction… 'blessed life'"': Schopenhauer, 1988, p. 141.
p. 109f 'Every finite being… several others': cf Spinoza, *Ethica* IV.
p. 110 'Peace of mind… degree of suffering': cf Lütkehaus, 2008.
p. 111 'This form of life… *unfree*': by Spinoza in part IV of his *Ethica*.
p. 112 'Without the development… actually *are* it, too': This is the double-aspect theory of the mental and the physical, represented in Western philosophy by Spinoza and Schopenhauer, amongst others.
p. 114 'The feelings of pride… David Hume realized': Hume, 1978, pp. 277–80.
p. 115 'This means that the ability… "I" correctly': Anscombe, 1975.
p. 117f 'The need to see… part of our blood': Gendlin, 1997, p. 1f.
p. 122 '"If by eternity… lives in the present"': Wittgenstein, *Tractatus*, 6.4311.
p. 122 '"I myself am eternity… God in me"': Angelus Silesius, 1984, p.13.
p. 124 'The practices of… left hand': cf Walther, 2001.
p. 124 'indeed, the ability… mental activity': Aristotle, 1982, 980a21–b21.
p. 127 '"O Man… a thousand lives"': Angelus Silesius, 1984, pp. 24–27.
p. 130 'This is why Spinoza… but death': Spinoza, *Ethica* IV, Proposition 67; cf fn 38.
p. 131 'If, as Aristotle… an impoverished one': Aristotle, 1979, 1100; see also Nussbaum, 1999, pp. 49–59.

Chapter Four

p. 136 '"I don't know… prefer to leave it": Kertész, 2006, p. 76f.
p. 137 '"For this very context… question of murder"': Kertész, 2006, p. 207.
p. 138 '"It seems that neither… not important"': Kertész, 2006, p. 232. My italics.
p. 140 '"For there is no… unintelligible"': Hobbes, 1984, p. 48.
p. 140f 'In Werner Herzog's… collectively to a goal': Herzog, 1974.
p. 142 'Freud's treatment… last treatise on happiness"': Hennig Ritter in the *Frankfurter Allgemeine Zeitung*, 5/5/2006.
p. 143 '"Civilisation… conquered city"': Freud, 1948, p. 483.
p. 143f '"Freud expresses the same… naturally pacifistic"': Freud, 1950, p. 26.
p. 144 'According to Freud… object of their desire': Freud, 1959, p. 20.
p. 144 'But according to Freud… "portion of security"': Freud, 1948, p. 499.
p. 145 '"Life as it is set out… unsolvable tasks"': Ibid.
p. 148 'Freud believes… without "authentication"': Freud, 1948, p. 354.
p. 152 '"Once we have recognized… erotic illusions?"': Freud, 1948, p. 356.
p. 152f '"There is no agency… to another person?"': Freud, 1948, p. 351.

p. 153 'It has already been noted... conquered city"': Freud, 1948, p. 483.
p. 154 '"It... does... sense of guilt"': Freud, 1948, p. 493. My italics.
p. 155 '"The aggression of the conscience... authority"': Freud, 1948, p. 492.
p. 155f '"Every denial of a drive... further denials of our drives"': Freud, 1948, p. 488.
p. 156 'This is an image... police officers': Burgess, 1992, p. 190f.
p. 157 'Religious conflicts... psychoanalytical notion': cf Kakar, 1997.
p. 158 'Occasionally, Freud... enthusiasm for war': Freud, 1987, pp. 375–488.
p. 159 '"Thus... the two urges... individual at present"': Freud, 1948, p. 501.
p. 160f '"The cultural super-ego... neighbour as thyself"': Freud, 1948, p. 503.
p. 161 'Normal cultural activity... revision of this': cf Hampe, 2006b, pp. 93–110.
p. 161f 'In his psychoanalysis of civilization... eliminate the problem"': Freud, 1948, p. 503.
p. 162 '"The fateful question... self-destruction"': Freud, 1948, p. 506.
p. 163 'The best biological... quest for power': cf Nietzsche, 1955, Vol. II, pp. 838–900.
p. 163f 'From a historical... non-human time': cf Gould XXX.
p. 166 *The Beautiful Picture*: Jandl, 1983, p. 83.

Chapter Five

p. 167f 'From a purely theoretical... "God"': James, 1945, pp. 442f, 455.
p. 169 'Reference was once made... "nothing could happen" to you': Wittgenstein, 1989, p. 14f.
p. 170 'This balance... for each person': Whitehead, 1978, p. 111f.
p. 172 '"Initially people... of objects"': Cassirer, 1996, p. 175.
p. 175 'It is not only clown sketches... not a joke': Collins/Pinch, 2000, Ch. 2.
p. 176f 'What has also happened... tight-knit': Latour, 1995 and 2008.
p. 177f 'If adjustments... *hybrid collective*': Latour 1995 and 2001.
p. 181 '"Insistence on birth... trick of evil"': Whitehead 1929/1978, pp. 223.
p. 183 'The world of modern... threats to identity': cf Sennett, 1988, Ch. 7.
p. 183 'For if people... increases in importance': cf Hampe, 2006a, pp. 104–12.
p. 184 'A popular option... more significant': Nietzsche, 1969, pp. 445–531.
p. 190 'Some hymnal poems... a happy moment': cf, for example, *Der Bagger*, *Die Kröte* and *Der Fuchs* in Kühn, 2000.

Chapter Six

p. 207 'In the conversation... limits of human reason"': Nietzsche, 1955, Vol. II, p. 1222.
p. 211 'Bakhtin then developed... less in philosophy': cf Eilenberger, 2008.
p. 213f 'The presentation or demonstration... complexities of reality': Schulte, 1990, pp. 11–42.
p. 215 'If philosophy could align... prerequisite of human happiness': Cavell, 2004, p. 381.

BIBLIOGRAPHY

Angelus Silesius (Johannes Scheffler), *Cherubinischer Wandersmann*, critical edition, ed. Louise Gnädinger, Stuttgart, 1984.

Anscombe, Gertrude Elizabeth Margaret, 'The First Person', in S. Guttenplan (ed.), *Mind and Language*, Oxford, 1975, pp. 45–64.

Ariès, Philippe, *L' homme devant la mort*, Paris, 1978.

Aristotle, *Politik*, trans. and ed. Olof Gigon, Zurich, 1971.

Aristotle, *Nikomachische Ethik*, trans. and with a commentary by Franz Dirlmeier, Vol. 6, Berlin 1979.

Aristotle, *Metaphysik*. Greek/German, trans. H. Bonitz, Hamburg, 1982.

Bakhtin, Mikhail, *Probleme der Poetik Dostojewskis*, Munich, 1971.

Bhagavadgita, ed. Helmuth von Glasenapp, Stuttgart, 1986.

Beckett, Samuel, *Warten auf Godot*, Frankfurt am Main, 1960.

Blumenberg, Hans, *Lebenszeit und Weltzeit*, Frankfurt am Main, 2001.

Boole, George, *An Investigation of the Laws of Thought on which are founded the mathematical Theories of Logic and Probabilities*, New York, 1958.

Boyd, Richard N. 'Realism, Underdetermination, and a Causal Theory of Evidence', in *Nous*, Vol. 7, No. 1 (1973), pp. 1–12.

Bröcker, Walther, 'Rückblick auf Heidegger' in *Allgemeine Zeitschrift für Philosophie*, Vol. 26 (1977), No. 2, pp. 24–28.

Burgess, Anthony, *A Clockwork Orange*, Stuttgart, 1992.

Carnap, Rudolf, *Der logische Aufbau der Welt*, 1928 (reprint), Frankfurt am Main, Berlin and Vienna, 1979.

Cassirer, Ernst, *Substanzbegriff und Funktionsbegriff. Untersuchungen über die Grundlagen der Erkenntniskritik*, Berlin, 1910.

Cassirer, Ernst, 'Form und Technik', in: Peter Fischer (ed.), *Technikphilosophie. Von der Antike bis zur Gegenwart*, Leipzig, 1996.

Cavell, Stanley, *Cities of Words. Pedagogical Letters on a Register of the Moral Life*, Cambridge/Mass. and London, 2004.

Cavell, Stanley, *Philosophy the Day after Tomorrow*, Cambridge/Mass. and London, 2005.

Collins, Harry, and Pinch, Trevor, *Der Golem der Technologie. Wie die Wissenschaft unsere Wirklichkeit konstruiert*, Berlin, 2000.

Dewey, John, *Logic. The Theory of Inquiry*, New York, 1938.

Dostoyevsky, Fyodor, *Die Brüder Karamasow*, trans. Werner Creutzinger, Berlin and Weimar, 1986.

Driesch, Hans, *Philosophie des Organischen*, Gifford Lectures given at Aberdeen University in 1907–1908, Leipzig, 1909.

Eilenberger, Wolfram, *Das Werden des Menschen im Wort. Eine Studie zur Kulturphilosophie Michail M. Bachtins*, Zurich, 2008.

Elias, Norbert, *Über die Einsamkeit der Sterbenden in unseren Tagen*, Frankfurt am Main, 1982.

Elias, Norbert, *Engagement und Distanzierung*, Frankfurt am Main, 1983.

Epictetus, *Handbüchlein der Moral und Unterredungen*, ed. Heinrich Schmidt, Stuttgart, 1984.

Feyerabend, Paul, *Against Method. Outline of an Anarchistic Theory of Knowledge*, London, 1975.

Foerster, Heinz von, *Sicht und Einsicht. Versuche einer operativen Erkenntnistheorie*, authorised German edition by Wolfram K. Köck, Brunswick and Wiesbaden, 1985.

Freud, Sigmund, *Das Unbehagen in der Kultur*, in Idem.,*Gesammelte Werke*, Vol. XIV, *Werke aus den Jahren 1925–1931*, Frankfurt am Main and London, 1948, pp. 419–506.

Freud, Sigmund, *Die Zukunft einer Illusion*, in Idem., *Gesammelte Werke*, Vol. XIV, *Werke aus den Jahren 1925–1931*, Frankfurt am Main and London, 1948, pp. 323–80.

Freud, Sigmund, *Warum Krieg?*, in: Idem., *Gesammelte Werke*, Vol. XVI, *Werke aus den Jahren 1932–1939*, Frankfurt am Main and London, 1950, pp. 11–29.

Freud, Sigmund, *Entwurf einer Psychologie*, in Idem., *Gesammelte Werke*, supplementary volume, Frankfurt am Main, 1987, pp. 375–488.

Gehlen, Arnold, *Die Seele im technischen Zeitalter. Sozialpsychologische Probleme in der industriellen Gesellschaft*, Hamburg, 1957.

Gendlin, Eugene T., *A Process Model*, Chicago, 1997.

Gilbert, William, *De Magnete*, trans. Paul Fleury Mottelay, New York, 1958.

Geuss, Raymond, *Outside Ethics*, Princeton and Oxford, 2005.

Gould, Stephen Jay, *Time's Arrow, Time's Cycle: Myth and Metaphor in the Discovery of Geological Time*, Cambridge/Mass, 1987.

Grassmann, Hermann, 'Zur Theorie der Farbmischung', in *Poggendorfs Annalen der Physik und Chemie*, Vol. 89 (1853), pp. 69–84.

Groeben, Norbert, 'Die Inhalts-Struktur-Trennung als konstantes Dialog-Konsens-Prinzip?', in B. Scheele (ed.), *Struktur-Lege-Verfahren als Dialog-Konsens-Methodik. Ein Zwischenfazit zur Forschungsentwicklung bei der rekonstruktiven Erhebung Subjektiver Theorien*, Münster, 1992, pp. 42–89.

Hagner, Michael and Rheinberger, Hans-Jörg, 'Experimental Systems, Objects of Investigation and Spaces of Representation' in Michael Heidelberger und Friedrich Steinle (eds.), *Experimental Essays – Versuche zum Experiment*, Baden-Baden, 1998, pp. 325–354.

Hagner, Michael, 'Gedankenlesen, Gehirnspiegel, Neuroimaging. Einblick ins Gehirn oder in den Geist?', in Idem., *Der Geist bei der Arbeit. Historische Untersuchungen zur Hirnforschung*, Göttingen, 2006.

Hampe, Michael, *Gesetz und Distanz. Über die Prinzipien der Gesetzmässigkeit in der neueren theoretischen und praktischen Philosophie*, Heidelberg, 1996.

Hampe, Michael, 'Unser Glaube an die Existenz abwesender Tatsachen', in Jens Kulenkampff (ed.), *David Hume. Eine Untersuchung über den menschlichen Verstand*, Berlin, 1997, pp. 73–94.

Hampe, Michael, *Die Macht des Zufalls. Vom Umgang mit dem Risiko*, Berlin, 2006a.

Hampe, Michael, 'Psychoanalyse als antike Philosophie: Stanley Cavells Freud', in Gugerli et al. (eds.), *Nach Feierabend.* Zürcher Jahrbuch für Wissensgeschichte 2: *Die Suche nach der eigenen Stimme*, Zurich and Berlin, 2006b, pp. 93–110.

Hampe, Michael, *Kleine Geschichte des Naturgesetzbegriffs*, Frankfurt am Main, 2007.

Hegel, Georg Wilhelm Friedrich, *Phänomenologie des Geistes* (1807), *Werke*, ed. Eva Moldenhauer and Karl Markus Michel, Vol. 3, Frankfurt am Main, 1986.

Hennetmair, Karl Ignaz, *Ein Jahr mit Thomas Bernard. Das versiegelte Tagebuch 1972*, Salzburg, 2000.

Herzog, Werner, *Kaspar Hauser. Jeder für sich und Gott gegen alle*, 1974.

Hobbes, Thomas, *Leviathan*, ed. Richard Tuck, Cambridge, 1991.

Hobbes, Thomas, *Leviathan oder Stoff, Form und Gewalt eines kirchlichen und bürgerlichen Staates*, ed. with an introduction by Iring Fetscher, trans. Walter Euchner, Frankfurt am Main, 1984.

Hölderlin, Friedrich, *Hyperion oder Der Eremit in Griechenland. Sämtliche Werke*, ed. Friedrich Beissner, Vol. 3, Stuttgart, 1958.

Hossenfelder, Malte (ed.), *Antike Glückslehren. Kynismus, Kyrenaismus, Stoa, Epikureismus und Skepsis.* Sources in German translation, Stuttgart, 1996.

Houellebecq, Michel, *Extension du domaine de la lutte*, Paris, 1994.

Hume, David, *A Treatise of Human Nature*, Oxford, 1978.

Hume, David, *Enquiry Concerning Human Understanding*, Oxford, 1975.

Hume, David, *Dialogues Concerning Natural Religion*, New York, 1948.

James, William, *The Varieties of Religious Experience. A Study in Human Nature*, ed. and with an introduction by Martin E. Marty, London, 1985.

Jandl, Ernst, *Selbstportrait des Schachspielers als trinkende Uhr. Gedichte*, Darmstadt, 1983.

Jankélévitch, Vladimir, *Der Tod*, trans. from the French by Brigitta Restorff, Frankfurt am Main, 2005.

Jankélévitch, Vladimir, *Vorlesung über Moralphilosophie*. Notes from 1962–1963 at the Free University of Brussels, ed. Françoise Schwab, trans. from the French by Jürgen Brankel, Vienna, 2007.

Kakar, Sudhir, *Die Gewalt der Frommen*, Munich, 1997.

Kertész, Imre, *Dossier K. Eine Ermittlung*, Reinbek bei Hamburg, 2006.

Köhlmeier, Michael, *Abendland*, Munich, 2007.

Kühn, Johannes, *Mit den Raben am Tisch: ausgewählte und neue Gedichte*, Munich, 2000.

Kuhn, Thomas S., *The Structure of Scientific Revolutions*, Chicago, 1962.

Latour, Bruno, *Wir sind nie modern gewesen*, Frankfurt am Main, 1995.

Latour, Bruno, 'Haben auch Objekte eine Geschichte? Ein Zusammentreffen von Pasteur und Whitehead in einem Milchsäurebad', in Michael Hagner (ed.), *Ansichten der Wissenschaftsgeschichte*, Frankfurt am Main, 2001, pp. 272–296.

Latour, Bruno, *Von der Realpolitik zur Dingpolitik*, Berlin, 2005.

Latour, Bruno, '"It's the development, stupid!" or How to modernize Modernization?', in Jim Proctor (ed.), *Postenvironmentalism*, Cambridge/Mass., 2008.

Lewin, Kurt, *Der Übergang von der aristotelischen zur galileischen Denkweise in Biologie und Psychologie* in *Kurt-Lewin-Werkausgabe*, Vol. 1, ed. Alexandre Métraux, Bern and Stuttgart, 1981, pp. 233–278.

Laudan, Larry, 'A Confutation of Convergent Realism', in *Philosophy of Science*, Vol. 48, No. 1 (1981), pp. 19–49.

Leibniz, Gottfried Wilhelm, *Essais de théodicée. Sur la bonté de dieu, la liberté de l'homme et l'origine du mal/Die Theodizee. Von der Güte Gottes, der Freiheit des Menschen und dem Ursprung des Übels*, Philosophische Schriften, Vol. II, ed. and trans. Herbert Herring, Darmstadt, 1985.

Lorenz, Kuno, 'Nāgājuna (ca. 120–200 n. Chr.) und Śaa. mkara (ca. 670–740 n. Chr.)' in Otfried Höffe (ed.), *Klassiker der Philosophie 1. Von den Vorsokratikern bis David Hume*, Munich, 2008, pp. 127–141.

Lütkehaus, Ludger, *Vom Anfang und Ende. Zwei Essays*, Frankfurt am Main, 2008.

Marx, Karl, 'Aus den Exzerptheften: die entfremdete und die unentfremdete Gesellschaft, Geld, Kredit und Menschlichkeit', in *Marx-Engels-Studienausgabe II*, ed. Iring Fetscher, Hamburg, 1966.

Michaelis, Edgar, *Einleitung zu Carl Gustav Carus' 'Vorlesung über Psychologie'*, Darmstadt, 1958.

Meister Eckehart, *Deutsche Predigten und Traktate*, ed. and trans. Josef Quint, Stuttgart, 1976.

Miller, David, 'Popper's Qualitative Theory of Verisimilitude', in *The British Journal for the Philosophy of Science*, Vol. 25 (1974), No. 2, pp. 166–177.

Moore, George Edward, *Principia Ethica*, Cambridge, 1903.

Morrison, James, 'Vico's Principle of Verum is Factum and the Problem of Historicism', in *Journal of the History of Ideas*, Vol. 39/4 (1978), pp. 579–595.

Muschg, Adolf, *Literatur als Therapie? Ein Exkurs über das Heilsame und das Unheilbare*. Frankfurt lectures, Frankfurt am Main, 1981.

Nádas, Péter, *Der eigene Tod*, trans. from the Hungarian by Heinrich Eisterer, Göttingen, 2002.

Newton, Isaac, *Theological Manuscripts*, selected, ed. and with an introduction by Herbert MacLachlan, Liverpool, 1950.

Nietzsche, Friedrich, *Die fröhliche Wissenschaft*, in Idem., *Werke in drei Bänden*, ed. Karl Schlechta, Munich, 1955, pp. 7–274.

Nietzsche, Friedrich, *Die Genealogie der Moral* in Idem., *Werke in drei Bänden*, ed. Karl Schlechta, Munich, 1955, pp. 761–900.

Nietzsche, Friedrich, *Der Antichrist. Fluch auf das Christentum* in Idem., *Werke in drei Bänden*, ed. Karl Schlechta, Munich, 1955, pp.1160–1235.

Nietzsche, Friedrich, *Umwertung aller Werte*. Compiled from Nietzsche's literary estate and ed. by Friedrich Würzbach, Munich, 1969.

Niiniluoto, Ilkka, und Tuomela, Raimo (ed.), *The Logic and Epistemology of Scientific Change*, *Acta Philosophica Fennica*, Vol. 30, Helsinki, 1979.

Niiniluoto, Ilkka, 'Scientific Progress', in *Stanford Encyclopedia of Philosophy*, Version 26/2/2007.

Nuland, Sherwin B., *How We Die*, New York, 1993.

Nussbaum, Martha, *Gerechtigkeit oder das gute Leben*, Frankfurt am Main, 1999.

Parfit, Derek, *Reasons and Persons*, Oxford, 1984.

Peirce, Charles Sanders, *8th Lowell Lecture*, in Idem., *The Collected Papers of Charles*

Sanders Peirce, ed. Charles Hartshorne und Paul Weiss, Cambridge/Mass., 1965, pp. 413–433.

Pircher, Wolfgang, 'Die Sprache des Ingenieurs', in David Gugerli et al. (eds.), *Nach Feierabend*. Zürcher Jahrbuch für Wissensgeschichte 1: *Bilder der Natur-Sprachen der Technik*, Zurich and Berlin, 2005, pp. 83–110.

Popper, Karl, *Conjectures and Refutations: The Growth of Scientific Knowledge*, London, 1963.

Popper, Karl, *Alles Leben ist Problemlösen: Über Erkenntnis, Geschichte und Politik*, Munich and Zurich, 1994.

Plato, *Timaios*, *Werke in acht Bänden*. Greek and German, ed. Gunter Eigler, Vol. 7, Darmstadt, 1972.

Plato, *Der Staat*, *Werke in acht Bänden*. Greek and German, ed. Gunter Eigler, Vol. 4, Darmstadt, 1972.

Psillos, Stathis, *Scientific Realism. How Science Tracks Truth*, London and New York, 1999.

Rheinberger, Hans-Jörg, 'Dimensionen der Darstellung in der Praxis des wissenschaftlichen Experimentierens', in Michael Hampe und Maria-Sibylla Lotter (eds.), '*Die Erfahrungen, die wir machen, sprechen gegen die Erfahrungen, die wir haben*'. *Über Formen der Erfahrung in den Wissenschaften*, Berlin, 2000, pp. 235–246.

Rohs, Peter, *Feld-Zeit-Ich. Entwurf einer feldtheoretischen Transzendentalphilosophie*, Frankfurt am Main, 1996.

Ros, Arno, *Begründung und Begriff. Wandlungen des Verständnisses begrifflicher Argumentation*. Vol II: *Neuzeit*, Hamburg, 1990.

Rousseau, Jean-Jacques, *Émile*, ed. Pierre-Maurice Masson, Paris, 1914.

Schöne, Albrecht, *Goethes Farbentheologie*, Munich, 1987.

Schopenhauer, Arthur, *Die Welt als Wille und Vorstellung*. In accordance with the definitive editions, ed. Ludger Lütkehaus, Two Vols., Zurich, 1988.

Schulte, Joachim, *Chor und Gesetz*, Frankfurt am Main, 1990.

Seel, Martin, *Versuch über die Form des Glücks. Studien zur Ethik*, Frankfurt am Main, 1999.

Sennett, Richard, *Flexible Man*, New Haven and London, 1998.

Spinoza, Baruch de, *Opera*, commissioned by the Heidelberg Academy of Sciences, ed. Carl Gebhardt, Four Vols., Heidelberg, 1925.

Spinoza, Baruch de, *Ethica/Ethik*, in Idem., *Opera/Werke*. Latin and German. Vol. 2. Ed. V. K. Blumenstock, Darmstadt, 1980.

Tarski, Alfred, 'The Semantic Conception of Truth', in Herbert Feigl und Wilfrid Sellars (eds.), *Readings in Philosophical Analysis*, New York, 1949, pp. 52–84.

Tarski, Alfred, 'Truth and Proof', in *Scientific American*, Vol. 220 (1969), pp. 63–77.

Thomä, Dieter, *Vom Glück in der Moderne*, Frankfurt am Main, 2003.

Tichy, Pavel, 'On Popper's Definitions of Verisimilitude', in *The British Journal for the Philosophy of Science*, Vol. 25 (1974), No. 2, pp. 155–160.

Toulmin, Stephen, und Goodfield, June, *The Fabric of the Heavens*, London, 1961.

Toulmin, Stephen, *Human Understanding*, Oxford, 1972.

Tugendhat, Ernst, *Anthropologie statt Metaphysik*, Munich, 2007.

Vico, Giambattista, *Cinque libri de' principj di una scienza nuova d'intorno alla commune natura delle nazioni*, Naples, 1730.

Walther, Wolfgang (ed.), *Koan-Sammlung 1 & 2*, Frankfurt am Main, 2001.

Weinberg, Steven, 'The Non-Revolution of Thomas Kuhn', in Idem., *Facing Up. Science and Its Cultural Adversaries*, Cambridge/Mass. and London, 2001.

Weizsäcker, Viktor von, *Pathosophie*. Gesammelte Schriften. Vol. 10, Frankfurt am Main, 2005.

Westfall, Richard S., *Never at Rest. A Biography of Isaac Newton*, Cambridge, 1980.

Whitehead, Alfred North, *Religion in the Making*, London, 1926, reprint New York, 1960.

Whitehead, Alfred North, *Process and Reality. An Essay in Cosmology*, Cambridge, 1929, eds. David Ray Griffin and Donald W. Sherburne, New York, 1978.

Wittgenstein, Ludwig, *Lectures and Conversations on Aesthetics, Psychology and Religious Belief*, ed. Cyril Barret, Oxford, 1966.

Wittgenstein, Ludwig, *Tractatus logico-philosophicus*, in Idem., *Schriften 1*, Frankfurt am Main, 1980, pp. 7–84.

Wittgenstein, Ludwig, *Philosophische Untersuchungen*, in Idem., *Schriften 1*, Frankfurt am Main, 1980, pp. 279–544.

Wittgenstein, Ludwig, *Vortrag über Ethik und andere kleine Schriften*, ed. Joachim Schulte, Frankfurt am Main, 1989.

Williams, Bernard, *Truth and Truthfulness. An Essay in Genealogy*, Princeton and Oxford, 2002.

Wolkenhauer, Olaf, 'Systems biology: The reincarnation of systems theory in applied biology?', in *Briefings in Bioinformatics*, Vol. 2(3) (2001), pp. 258–270.

Permissions

Epigraphs

p. vii

Cavell, Stanley, reprinted by permission of the publisher from *Cities of Words: Pedagogical Letters on a Register of the Moral Life* by Stanley Cavell, p. 381, Cambridge, Mass., The Belknap Press of Harvard University Press, Copyright © 2004 by the President and Fellows of Harvard College.

Geuss, Raymond, *Outside Ethics*, p. 239, © 2005 by Princeton University Press. Reprinted by permission of Princeton University Press.

Nāgārjuna's *Mūlamadhyamakakārikā*, Chap. XXIV, 10, in: *The Fundamental Wisdom of the Middle Way*, translated by Garfield (1996), 15 words from p. 298. By permission of Oxford University Press, USA.

Seelig, Carl, *Wanderungen mit Robert Walser*, © 1977 Suhrkamp Verlag GmbH & Co KG, Frankfurt. With kind permission of the 'Robert Walser-Zentrum' in Bern and Suhrkamp Verlag Berlin.

pp. 136–62

Based on the text: Michael Hampe, 'Die Psychoanalyse als Kulturphilosophie? Freud und das Unbehagen in der Kultur', from *Das Leben denken – Die Kultur denken*, Vol. 2: *Kultur*, ed. Ralf Konersmann, pp. 147–168. © Verlag Karl Alber GmbH, Freiburg/Munich 2007. Printed with the kind permission of Verlag Karl Alber GmbH.

A NOTE ON THE AUTHOR

Michael Hampe studied philosophy, psychology and literature in Heidelberg and Cambridge, where he ultimately earned his degree in biology with a focus on human biology and human genetics. He was a Visiting Professor at Trinity College, Dublin 1990–1992, Professor of Theoretical Philosophy at the University of Kassel from 1997–1999 and from 1999–2003, he was Professor of Philosophy at Otto Friedrich University, Bamberg. Since 2003, Michael Hampe has been Professor of Philosophy at Zurich's Swiss Federal Institute of Technology.